Hey! There's Math in My Literature!

Using Literature to Support Math Standards

Pamela Gunter
and
Justine Dunn
Illustrated by Becky Radtke

Rigby Best Teachers Press®
An imprint of Rigby®

Dedications and Acknowledgements

This book is dedicated to every student I have had in my classroom that has inspired me to teach, as well as my father, who was my first teacher. I also dedicate this book to my family, Ivan, Simone, and Sierra, who are *my* teachers of love and encouragement. Many thanks to Georgine Cooper who has encouraged me to write this book, and Tom, Mary, Carol, and Justine, who are a wonderful group to work with. I am proud to call them friends.

–Pam Gunter

I would like to dedicate this book to my husband, Ray, and to my mom, Nancy Williams. Many thanks to Georgine, Mary, and Carol for your support and friendship. It's been a great ride!

–Justine Dunn

www.HarcourtAchieve.com
1.800.531.5015

Editor: Mary Susnis
Executive Editor: Georgine Cooper
Designer: Biner Design
Design Production Manager: Tom Sjoerdsma
Cover Illustrator: Aaron Romo
Interior Illustrator: Becky Radtke

09 08 07 06 05 04
10 9 8 7 6 5 4 3 2 1

ISBN 0-7398-8474-3
Hey! There's Math in My Literature!

Printed in the United States of America

TABLE OF CONTENTS

Introduction

Literacy is often solely associated with reading; however, literacy *should* and *can* be taught throughout the school day and across the curriculum. *Hey! There's Math in My Literature!* is designed to help teachers combine quality children's literature with hands-on math activities. There is a wealth of quality children's literature that supports the connection between math and literacy. This resource provides suggestions for read-alouds and coordinating activities for teaching basic math skills, which are correlated to the standards set by the National Council for Teachers of Mathematics. The activities can also be used with other children's books or on their own. The *Suggested Math Literature List* on pages 91–92 can help you incorporate math into your classroom library.

> *Mathematics helps children make sense of the world around them and find meaning in the physical world. Through mathematics, children learn to understand their world in terms of numbers and shapes. They learn to reason, to connect ideas, and to think logically. Mathematics is more than the rules and operations we learned in school. It is about connections and seeing relationships in everything we do.*
>
> (Fromboluti and Rinck, 1999)

> *The teacher of mathematics should create a learning environment that fosters the development of each student's mathematical power by using the physical space and materials in ways that facilitate students' learning of mathematics; and by consistently expecting and encouraging students to work independently or collaboratively to make sense of mathematics.*
>
> (NCTM Standards, 2000)

Each literature selection will be accompanied by the following:

NCTM Standards

The National Council for Teachers of Mathematics (NCTM) standards can be found on the Internet at *http://standards.nctm.org*. It is important to become familiar with these standards as well as your district's standards and curriculum, as they should be used for instructional planning. In most schools, the teacher is able to decide how best to deliver instruction that meets the objectives set forth in the standards. Teachers should consider their own teaching style when creating activity plans based on standards. Because standards and benchmarks are crucial for educators today, each activity notes the specific NCTM standard(s) and skill(s) being addressed.

Math Vocabulary

Students should be familiar with math vocabulary so they can comprehend and discuss concepts. You will find a list of suggested math vocabulary words in each unit and on page 90. Post these words in your Math Center, around the room, or on a math bulletin board. Model how these words are used when discussing math concepts and encourage children to use these vocabulary words when they talk about math. Write the appropriate math vocabulary words on sentence strips and review the words before each unit.

Prereading Activity

The value of preparing students for reading has been recognized in professional literature since the turn of the 20th century. Research continues to support the practice of preparing students for reading and learning. (Readence, et. al., 2000) The *Prereading Activity* for each unit will help prepare the children and help you assess their background knowledge.

Read-Aloud Activity

The Read-Aloud Activities in this book are whole-group activities that integrate literacy and math. Reading aloud introduces children to quality literature in a pleasing and comfortable format. Read the featured children's book aloud and work with the children to help them complete the corresponding *Application and Practice* and *Extension Activity*.

Application and Practice Activity

"Practice makes perfect" sums up the necessity for children to use what they are learning. When possible, provide opportunities that allow children to use what they are learning in context rather than in isolation. For example, the *Application and Practice Activity* immediately follows the *Read-Aloud Activity*.

Extension Activity

Because children enter your room with many different academic levels, instruction should be modified to meet individual needs. The *Extension Activity* is a more challenging activity. If children master the *Application and Practice Activity,* this activity can be used to extend learning to a higher level.

Literacy Centers provide a wide variety of learning opportunities for children. You can foster children's mathematical development by providing environments rich in language, where thinking is encouraged, uniqueness is valued, and exploration is supported. Suggestions for activities in the following Literacy Centers are listed for each literature selection.

 **Reading/Writing**

 **Art**

 **Math**

 **Dramatic Play**

 **Science**

 **Kids in the Kitchen**

Caution: Some activities include using edible items. Always check for food sensitivities and allergies before serving food or allowing children to handle food.

Before each activity is presented, gather your children in a whole group to discuss and demonstrate appropriate behavior and procedures for Literacy Centers. Ask the children to help create guidelines for participating in the Literacy Centers and ask for volunteers to help demonstrate proper use of the materials in each center.

Five Minute Math Fun

Reinforcing concepts and skills can be accomplished in many ways. It is important to keep things interesting for your children. Too much practice on the same material in the same way can lead to boredom or frustration. *Five Minute Math Fun* is a quick whole-group reinforcement of the concepts and skills being addressed. It can also be used as an informal assessment.

Home Connection

Children learn best when they are interested and excited about what they are doing. Their interest and excitement doesn't have to end when they leave your classroom. One of the most important factors that can lead to a successful program is parental involvement. Not only can parents support your instructional efforts; they can reinforce and re-emphasize the strategies you share with children.

Send home the parent letter located in each unit in order to reinforce what you are doing in the classroom. All of the home activities in this book can be done during a child's daily routines. They require no special equipment or detailed planning. Parents can use them to do something pleasant with their child, add some interest to an otherwise routine activity, or to keep their children interested or occupied.

Send home the *Supply Request Letter* on page 89 the week prior to each unit. Parents are a wonderful resource and enjoy contributing to the classroom.

Scope and Sequence

Title	Math Skills	NCTM Standard	Page Numbers
Fish Eyes	Counting, Performing Simple Addition and Subtraction Operations	Number and Operations	10–18
Cubes, Cones, Cylinders, and Spheres	Identifying Shapes and Attributes, Sorting, Recognizing Symmetry	Geometry	19–29
Inch by Inch	Measuring, Predicting, Gathering and Recording Data	Measurement	30–36
Froggy Gets Dressed	Probability, Gathering and Recording Data, Graphing	Data Analysis and Probability	37–46
Give Me Half!	Understanding and Representing Basic Fractions	Number and Operations	47–53
Dave's Down-to-Earth Rock Shop	Classifying, Gathering and Recording Data, Sorting, Questioning	Data Analysis and Probability	54–59
Caps for Sale	Problem Solving, Sorting, Exploring Combinations,Gathering and Recording Data, Patterning	Problem Solving	60–67
The Grouchy Ladybug	Measuring Time, Gathering and Recording Data	Measurement	68–76
Pattern Fish	Patterning, Sequencing, Extending Patterns, Investigating	Reasoning and Proof	77–83

Ehlert, Lois. (1990). *Fish eyes.* New York: Harcourt Brace.

NCTM Standard: Number and Operations

"During the early years teachers must help students strengthen their sense of number, moving from the initial development of basic counting techniques to more sophisticated understandings of the size of numbers, number relationships, patterns, operations, and place value."

-NCTM Standards, 2000

In kindergarten through grade 2 all students should—

- count with understanding and recognize "how many" in sets of objects.
- connect number words and numerals to the quantities they represent, using various physical models and representations.
- understand the effects of adding and subtracting whole numbers.
- develop and use strategies for whole number computations, with a focus on addition and subtraction.
- use a variety of methods and tools to compute, including objects, mental computation, estimation, paper and pencil, and calculators.

Math Vocabulary

count	graph	add	subtract	plus
minus	equals	more	less	

Prereading Activity

- **Materials:** *Fish Eyes* by Lois Ehlert

Introduce the book *Fish Eyes* to the children and ask them to read the title and subtitle with you. Ask the children the following questions as you gain an understanding of their background knowledge. "What do you predict this book will be about?", "What does the author mean by 'A Book You Can Count On?'", "Why is it important to learn about counting?" Conduct a short demonstration using the children as manipulatives and show them how to *add* and *subtract*. For example, one child *plus* one child *equals* two children. Three children *minus* one child *equals* two children.

Read-Aloud Activity

- **Materials:** *Fish Eyes* by Lois Ehlert

Read *Fish Eyes* with the children. Ask them to think about the question at the end of the book. Discuss the different types of fish in the book and wait to see if the children notice how the eyes are a different color on each page. Discuss the words *fantailed, flipping, flashy,* and *darting.* As a whole group, *count* how many fish are in the book. Say each number as you point to the corresponding numeral and number word.

Application and Practice Activity

- **Materials:** small inflatable pool, paper fish pattern, page 16, one magnet per child, one dowel per child, one paper clip per child, string, math counters

Copy the paper fish pattern from page 16 and distribute one page to each child. Ask the children to color and cut out each fish. Write a number from 1-10 on each fish and attach a paper clip. The children can then put their fish in the pool. Tie one end of a string to the dowel and tie a magnet to the other end. The children can "go fishing" in the "pond." Ask them to "catch" fish and *add* the numbers together. They can use math counters if needed. Then ask the children to put one fish back into the pond and *subtract* that number from the total. Assist as needed.

Extension Activity

- **Materials:** one paper cup per child, 10 fish crackers per child, one piece of blue construction paper per child, *Fish Eyes* by Lois Ehlert

<u>Caution:</u> This activity uses edible items. Always check for food sensitivities and allergies before serving food or allowing children to handle food.

Give each child a paper cup with 10 fish crackers and a piece of blue construction paper, to act as water. Each page of *Fish Eyes* has an addition problem at the bottom. Read the sentence as the children put the appropriate number of fish crackers on their paper. The children can then count all the fish on their mat to find the answer. Repeat this process for each addition problem and assist when necessary.

Reading/Writing: Fish Wishes

- **Materials:** Fish Pattern, page 16, pencils, tape, chart paper, marker

Prior to the activity, copy the Fish Pattern from page 16 for each child. The children can answer the author's question at the end of the book. They can write their answers (yes or no and a short explanation) on a paper fish. Prior to the activity, make a larger version of the chart pictured here. The children can put tape on the back of their fish and *graph* their responses. The children can *count* the yes and no responses and determine which response has *more* and which has *less*.

Do you wish to be a fish?

yes	no

Math: Egg Carton Math

- **Materials:** 4-5 egg cartons, small round stickers, marker, fish crackers

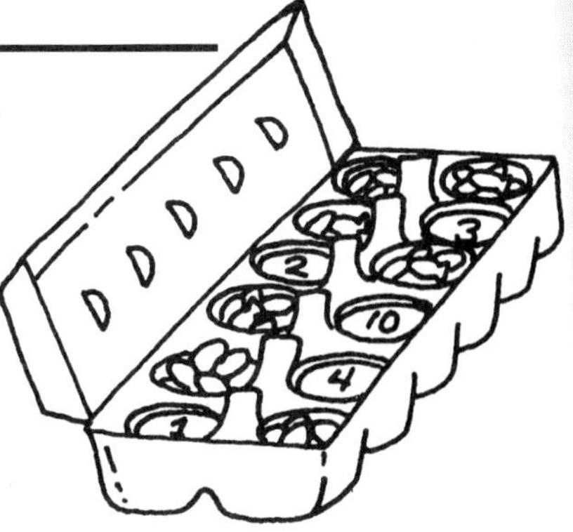

Caution: This activity uses edible items. Always check for food sensitivities and allergies before serving food or allowing children to handle food.

Prior to the activity, write the numbers 1-10 on small round stickers and attach them to the bottom of the inside of each egg carton. Children can read the number and place the corresponding number of fish crackers in the egg carton. Repeat this activity using the numbers 11-20, multiples of 2 or 5, or all even or odd numbers. The children will enjoy snacking on their fish crackers when they have finished.

Science: Ocean Sensory

- **Materials:** sensory table, water, blue food coloring, green shredded plastic grass, sand, shells, small plastic sea life creatures

Prior to the activity, fill your sensory table with water and add a few drops of blue food coloring and the ingredients listed above. The children will enjoy exploring the ocean in their classroom!

Art: Fishbowl Fun

- **Materials:** Fishbowl Patterns, pages 17–18, blue cellophane or plastic wrap, sea life rubber stamps or stickers, tape, scissors

Prior to the activity, copy the front and back fishbowl patterns on pages 17–18 for each child. The children will color and cut out their fishbowls. The front of the fishbowl will also be cut out. Children can then decorate the back of their fishbowl with the stamps or stickers. Using tape, the children will attach the blue cellophane or plastic behind the front of the fishbowl, and attach the front and back of the fishbowl together.

Dramatic Play: One, Two, Three, Four

- **Materials:** none needed

The children can count things in the dramatic play area, such as their friends, or all of the hats and shoes. They can also count how many children are wearing a particular color.

Kids in the Kitchen: Sea Snack

- **Materials:** one graham cracker per child, blue frosting, plastic knives, fish crackers, brown sugar

Caution: ***This activity uses edible items. Always check for food sensitivities and allergies before serving food or allowing children to handle food.***

If you cannot find blue frosting, mix a few drops of blue food coloring in some white frosting. Store in an airtight container until ready for use. To make this tasty treat, the children will spread the blue frosting (water) on the graham cracker and add fish crackers and a small amount of brown sugar (sand).

Five Minute Math Fun: Skip Counting

- **Materials:** large ball

This is a great outdoor activity, weather permitting. If needed, you can use the school gymnasium for the activity. Ask the children to form a circle. You will start by explaining that you are going to "skip count." Skip counting is counting forwards or backwards in multiples of a given number. Start with skip counting by twos. You will say "two" and gently bounce the ball to a child in the circle, who will catch it and say the next number in the sequence, which is four. Continue until all children have had a turn.

Home Connection

Copy the Parent Letter on page 15 and send it home the week you are conducting this unit.

Date:

Dear Parents:

This week in math, we are working on counting and simple addition and subtraction. We read the book *Fish Eyes* by Lois Ehlert and talked about if we wish to be a fish. We played in the ocean in our classroom, which was made by putting blue water in our sensory table. We added green shredded plastic grass that felt like seaweed!

You can help your child with counting and simple operations while doing everyday tasks. Here are some suggestions:

- Help your child count the silverware or practice adding one more as they set the table.
- Ask your child to count the buttons on shirts, coats, sweaters or pants.
- Visit a pet store and count the fish in each aquarium.
- Create simple addition and subtraction problems while at the grocery store, such as "I have two cans of soup in the cart. If I add three more, how many will I have?"

Early childhood experts Carol Sue Fromboluti and Natalie Rinck tell us, "Children's development is nourished through everyday play and explorations of the world around them. Therefore, it is important that families support young children's learning and play, answer their questions ... and stir their natural curiosity in order to lay foundations for success in school and beyond."

I look forward to your participation in our learning experiences.

Sincerely,

Fish Patterns

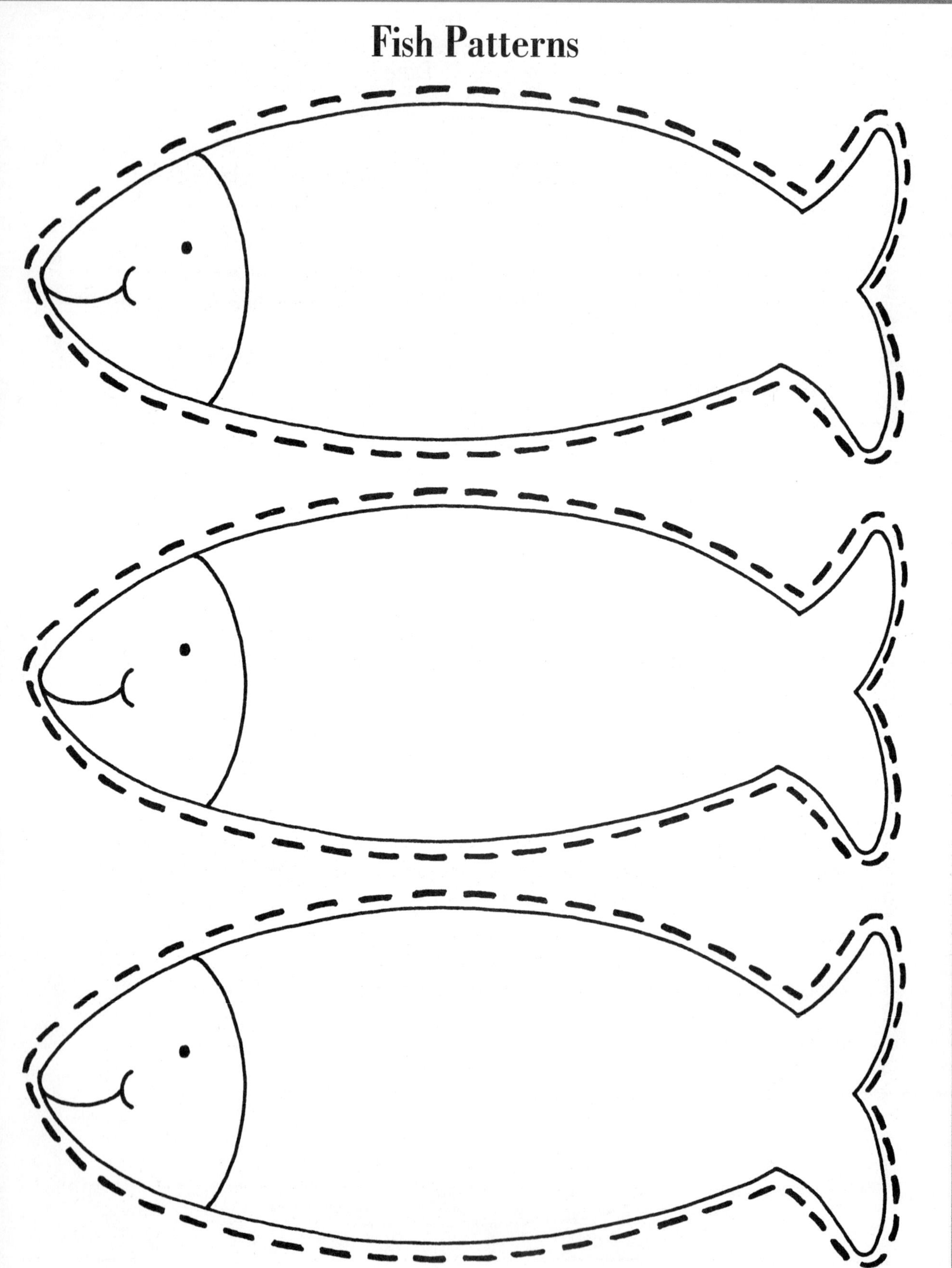

Fishbowl Pattern (front)

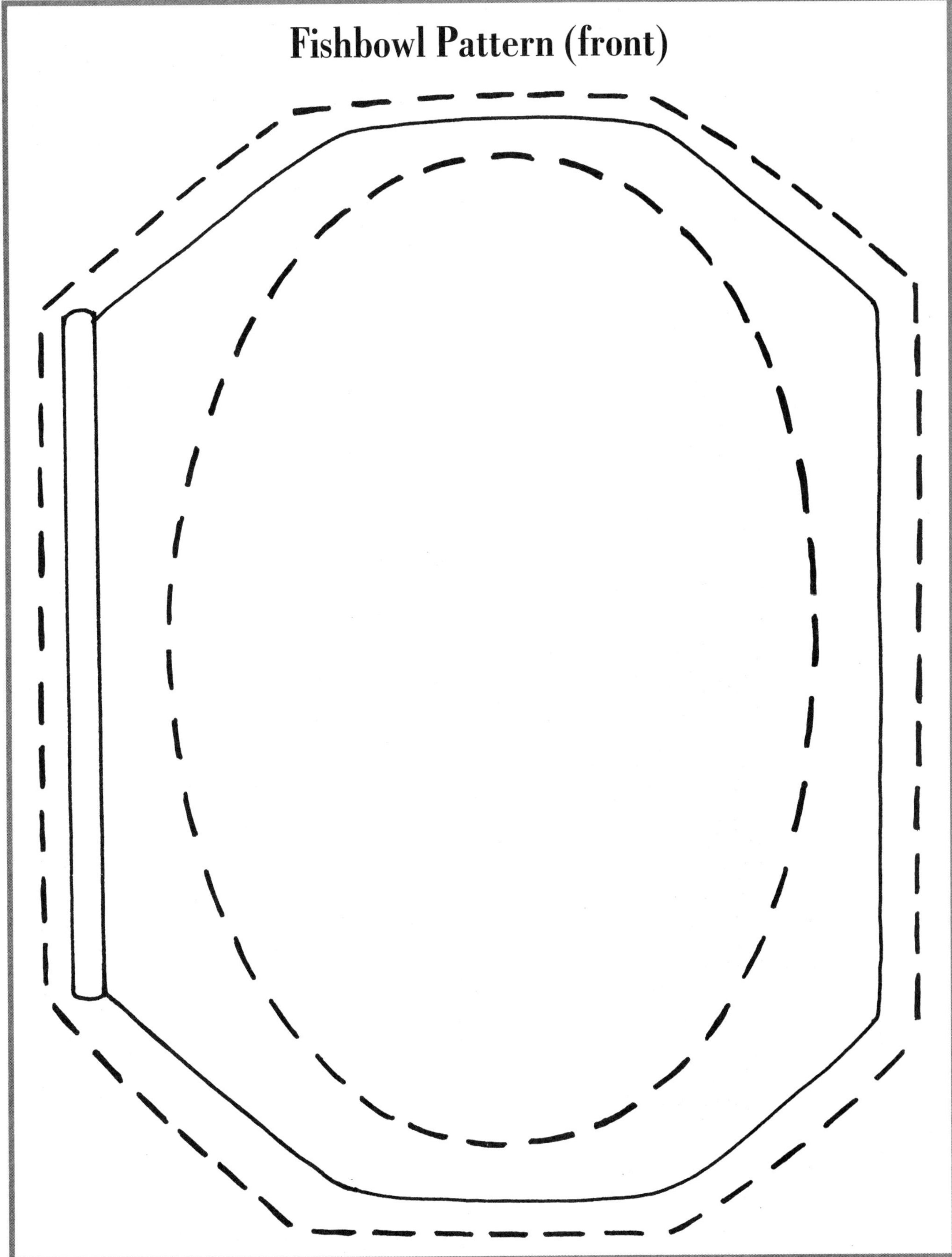

Fishbowl Pattern (back)

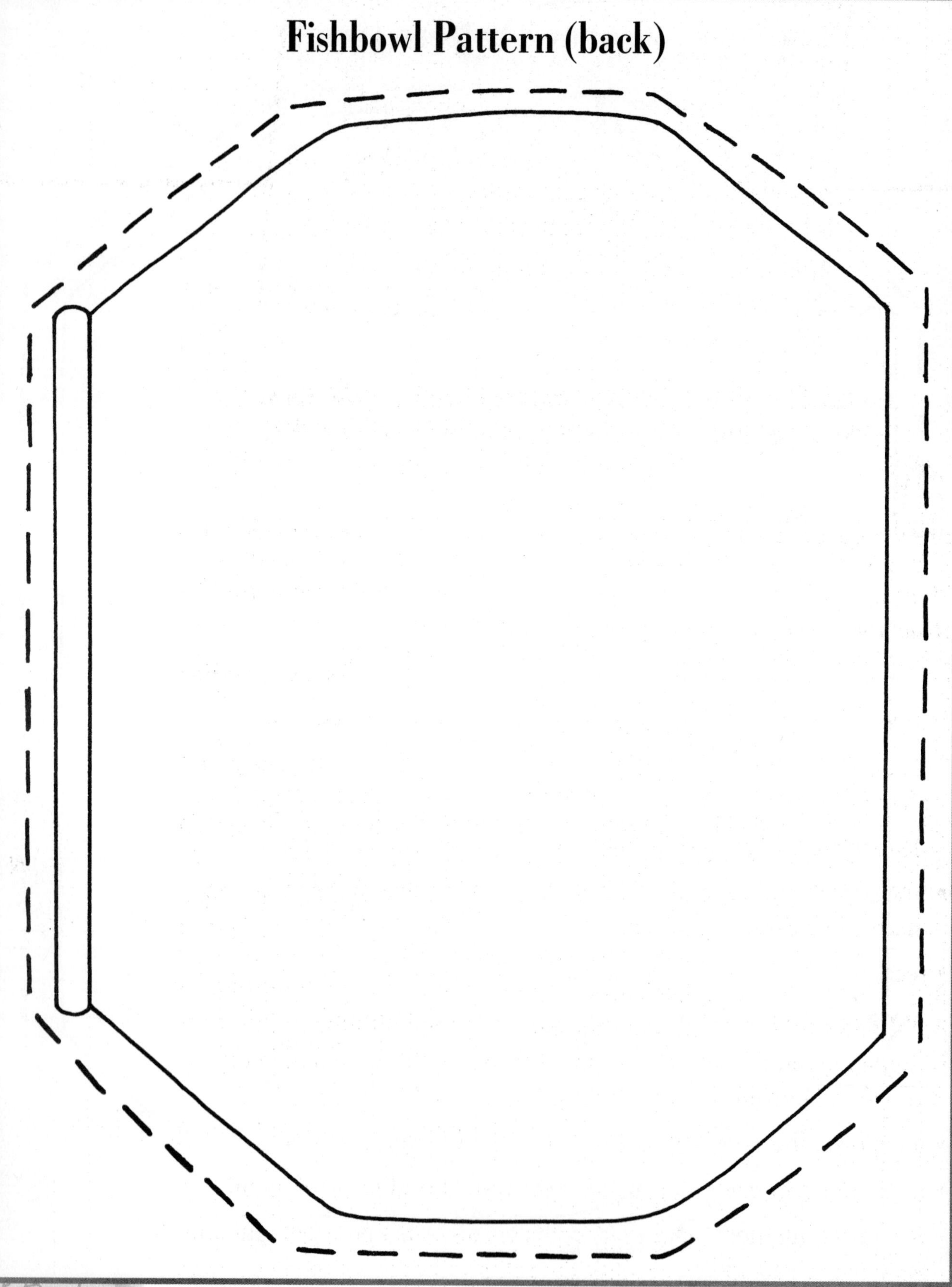

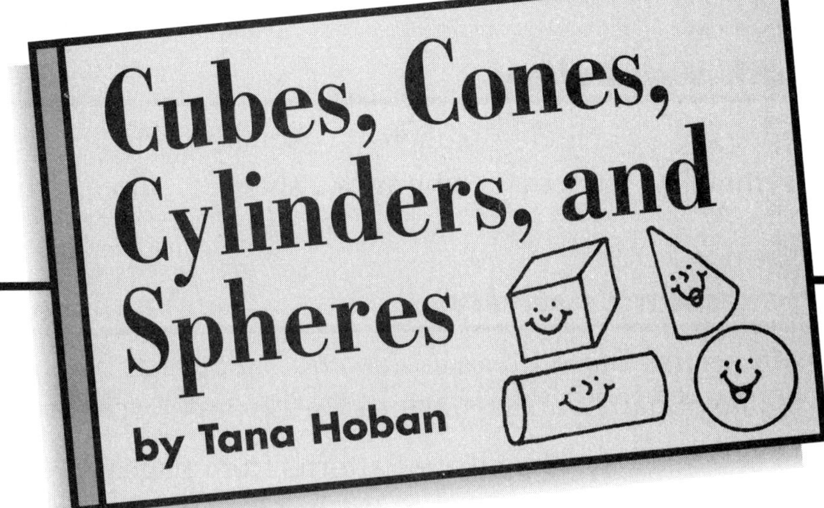

Hoban, Tana. (2000). *Cubes, cones, cylinders, and spheres.* New York: Greenwillow Books.

NCTM Standard: Geometry

"The geometric and spatial knowledge children bring to school should be expanded by explorations, investigations, and discussions of shapes and structures in the classroom."

-NCTM Standards, 2000

In prekindergarten through grade 2 all students should—

- recognize, name, build, draw, compare, and sort three-dimensional shapes.
- describe attributes and parts of three-dimensional shapes.
- investigate and predict the results of putting together and taking apart three dimensional shapes.
- recognize and apply slides, flips, and turns.
- recognize and create shapes that have symmetry.
- create mental images of geometric shapes using spatial memory and spatial visualization.
- recognize and recreate shapes from different perspectives.
- relate ideas in geometry to ideas in number and measurement.
- recognize geometric shapes and structures in the environment and specify their location.

Math Vocabulary

cube	cone	cylinder	sphere	square	circle	rectangle
triangle	symmetry	shapes	tangram	slide	flip	turn

Prereading Activity

- **Materials:** *Cubes, Cones, Cylinders, and Spheres* by Tana Hoban, Shape Patterns, pages 26–29, paper, scissors

Prior to the activity, copy the Shape Patterns from pages 26–29, one shape for each child. Read the title of the book aloud and ask the children what they know about these *shapes*. Explain that this book doesn't have words, but the pictures are very important. Distribute one shape to each child and ask him or her to cut out the shape. Discuss the shapes with the children and ask them to give an example of a similar shape that can be found in the environment.

Read-Aloud Activity

- **Materials:** *Cubes, Cones, Cylinders, and Spheres* by Tana Hoban, tangrams, shapes from the classroom environment: a cube, cone, cylinder and sphere, the children's shapes from the prereading activity

"Read" the story with the children, discussing their experiences with these *shapes*. Show the children the shapes from the classroom environment and ask them to identify each shape. Re-read the story and ask the children to hold up their shape if it corresponds to the picture shown. Discuss the attributes of these shapes and compare them to other shapes, such as a *circle, triangle, square,* and *rectangle*. Using *tangrams,* show the children how they can make shapes in the Math Center. Demonstrate and explain the vocabulary words *slide, flip,* and *turn*.

Application and Practice Activity

- **Materials:** Classroom Shape Search Activity, page 25, pencils or crayons

Prior to the activity, copy the Classroom Shape Search for the children. Ask them to walk around the classroom to search for shapes like those they saw in the book. The children can circle the shapes they find on their search. When all students have had a chance to find a few shapes, gather the group together and ask them to share their findings. If time allows, graph the results with the children.

Extension Activity

- **Materials:** one piece of 8" x 8" copy paper per child, soft clay, 4-5 small cardboard boxes in the shape of a cube, scissors, plastic knives, 4-5 small cardboard tubes (You may want to ask parents to contribute these materials.)

This activity will enable children to investigate and predict the results of putting together and taking apart shapes. The children will predict what each shape will look like when it is put together and taken apart.

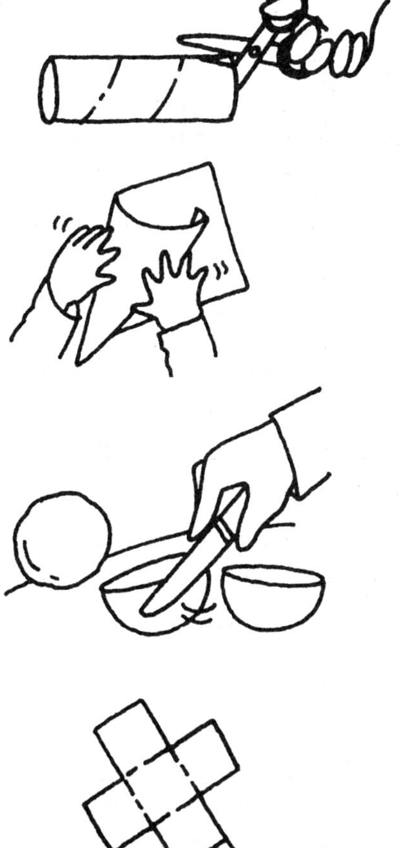

The children can use scissors to cut the tube in half lengthwise and open it. They can see what a *cylinder* looks like when it is taken apart.

The children can bring the opposite corners of the paper together into a *cone* shape and compare this shape to what the paper looked like before. Assist if necessary.

Each child can take some clay and roll it into a small ball that fits in the palm of his or her hand. This is an example of a *sphere*. The children can use a plastic knife to cut the sphere in half and see what it looks like.

The cardboard box is an example of a *cube*. The children can take apart the box and lay it flat.

Literacy Center Ideas

Reading/Writing: Geometry Groceries

- **Materials:** grocery advertisements, paper, pencils

Children can search for groceries in their favorite shape, write a grocery list, and categorize the items on their list by shape.

Math: Tangram Shapes

- **Materials:** tangrams, note cards

The children can create shapes using the tangrams as you demonstrated earlier. For extra support, create note cards that show some examples of how to make some shapes prior to the activity. Write the following vocabulary words on note cards as well: *slide, flip,* and *turn.*

Science: Sensory Measurement

- **Materials:** sensory table, water or sand, plastic or metal hollow shapes such as bowls, boxes, or cones

Using water or sand and some hollow objects of various shapes, children can estimate how many scoops of water or sand will fill each shape and test their guesses.

Art: Tactile Shapes

- **Materials:** shape templates, glue, scissors, sandpaper, aluminum foil, felt, rice, velvet material, furry material

The children can use shape templates to trace and cut out tactile shapes from various materials and make a collage with them if they choose. The children can also feel some of the tactile shapes with their eyes closed and try to guess the shape. If you do not have shape templates available, use the patterns on pages 26–29.

Dramatic Play: Shape Stretch

- **Materials:** large, plastic mat with colorful shapes, spinner with corresponding shapes

One child can spin the spinner and call out the colored shape. The other children can stretch their bodies to put a hand or foot on that shape on the plastic mat.

Kids in the Kitchen: Geometric Goodies

- **Materials:** bread, shape cookie cutters, cream cheese, peanut butter, butter, jelly, plastic knives

<u>Caution:</u> This activity uses edible items. Always check for food sensitivities and allergies before serving food or allowing children to handle food.

The children can use the shape cookie cutters to cut out shapes from the bread and use a plastic knife to put on their favorite spread.

Five Minute Math Fun: Symmetrical Shapes

- **Materials:** one piece of construction paper per child, pencils or crayons, scissors, shape templates

Explain to the children that they are going to make symmetrical shapes. Tell them that *symmetry* is shown when a shape looks exactly the same on both sides of a line or fold. Show the children how to fold their paper in half horizontally. The children can use the shape templates to trace and cut out a shape on the fold of the construction paper. Be sure to assist them when cutting so they don't cut out the fold. When they are finished, the children can unfold their paper and see the symmetrical shape they have created.

Home Connection

Copy the Parent Letter on page 24 and send it home the week you are conducting this unit.

Date:

Dear Parents:

This week in math, we are working on basic geometry skills, including identifying shapes and attributes, sorting, and symmetry. We read the book *Cubes, Cones, Cylinders, and Spheres* by Tana Hoban and talked about the shapes that are all around us. We made geometric goodies and tactile shapes and worked with tangrams.

You can help your child with basic geometry skills by helping to identify shapes in the environment. Here are some suggestions:

- Work on geometry skills with your child while putting away groceries. Your child can sort boxes, cans, fruits, and vegetables according to size and shape.
- Assist your child in making a creature or robot at home, using boxes, cones, dryer vent hose, and empty paper towel tubes of all sizes. The children may want to bring in their creations to share with the class and tell which shapes they used.
- Your child can do a shape search at home to find objects of various shapes and make a picture showing his or her findings.

Early childhood experts Carol Sue Fromboluti and Natalie Rinck remind us, "All children love to have things repeated even when they already know them, so don't hesitate to do things over and over again. In fact, repetition is how children practice what they are learning—and practice improves learning."

Together we are sending your child on the road to academic success. Thank you for your participation.

Sincerely,

Classroom Shape Search

Name: ______________________________

Circle the shapes you find in your classroom.

Draw a picture of each object you find.

cube	cone	cylinder	sphere
cube	cone	cylinder	sphere
cube	cone	cylinder	sphere
cube	cone	cylinder	sphere

Cube Template

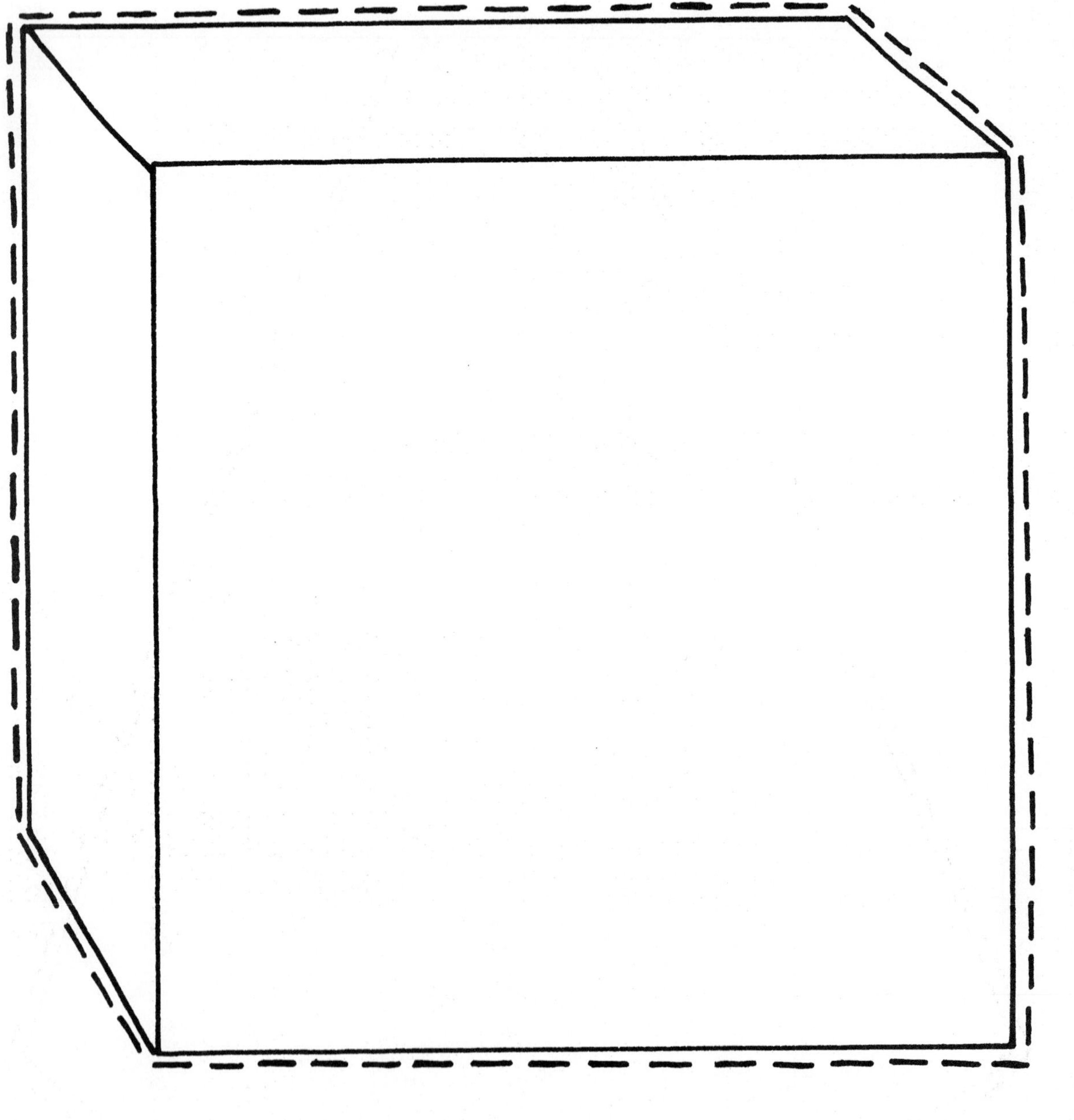

Cone Template

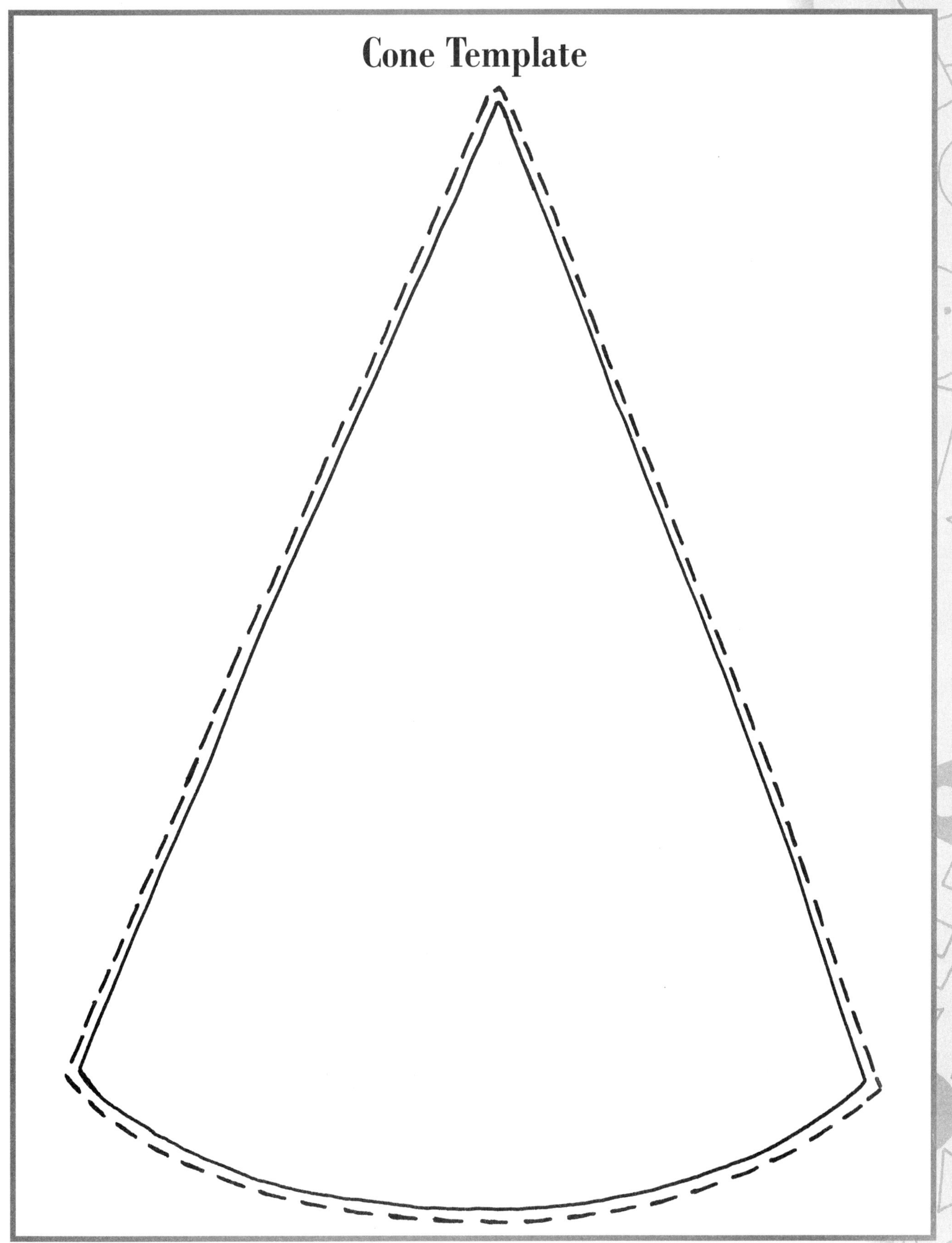

Cylinder Template

Sphere Template

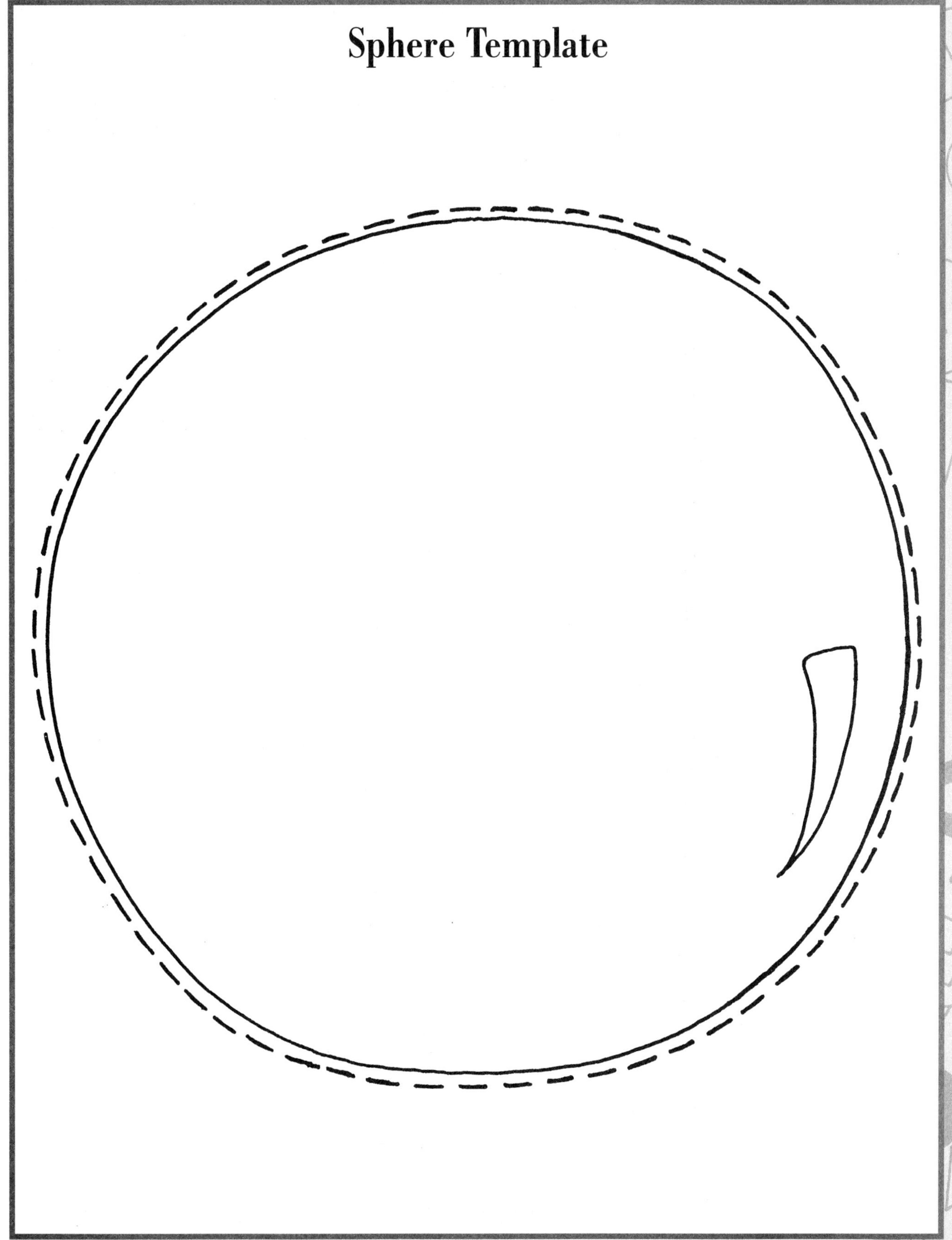

Lionni, Leo. (1960). *Inch by inch.*
New York: Astor-Honor Inc.

NCTM Standard: Measurement

"Teachers should guide students' experiences by making the resources for measuring available, planning opportunities to measure, and encouraging students to explain the results of their actions."

-NCTM Standards, 2000

In kindergarten through grade 2 all students should—

- recognize the attributes of length, volume, weight, area, and time.
- compare and order objects according to these attributes.
- understand how to measure using nonstandard and standard units.
- select an appropriate unit and tool for the attribute being measured.
- measure with multiple copies of units of the same size, such as paper clips laid end to end.
- use repetition of a single unit to measure something larger than the unit, for instance, measuring the length of a room using a standard meter stick.
- use tools to measure.

Math Vocabulary

measure	inch	length	longer	shorter	record
ruler	weigh	more	less	balance	scale

Prereading Activity

- **Materials:** *Inch by Inch* by Leo Lionni, ruler

Ask the children to help you read the title of the book. Ask them if anyone knows how long an *inch* is. Show the children an inch on a *ruler*. Tell them that a ruler is used to *measure*. Ask the children what kinds of things they can measure using a ruler.

Read-Aloud Activity

- **Materials:** *Inch by Inch* by Leo Lionni

Read *Inch by Inch* with the children. Ask the children to discuss what the inchworm did to avoid being eaten. Explain to the children that they are going to make inchworm books and measure items around their classroom.

Application and Practice Activity

- **Materials:** six $8\frac{1}{2}$" x 11" pieces of paper per child, stapler, Inchworm Patterns, page 36, scissors, crayons or markers, yarn,

Prior to the activity, six $8\frac{1}{2}$" x 11" sheets of paper in half and staple along the fold to make a blank book. Copy the Inchworm Patterns from page 36 for each child to color and cut out.
Because the children will be using the inchworms as a unit of measurement for several activities, consider laminating them for durability. Attach the inchworm to one end of a piece of yarn and staple the other end to the middle of the book. Model how the children can use their inchworm to measure items in the classroom. Ask students to draw the items they measure and *record* their findings in their inchworm books. If needed, direct students to specific items.

Extension Activity

• **Materials:** 4-5 shoeboxes, yarn, beads, scissors

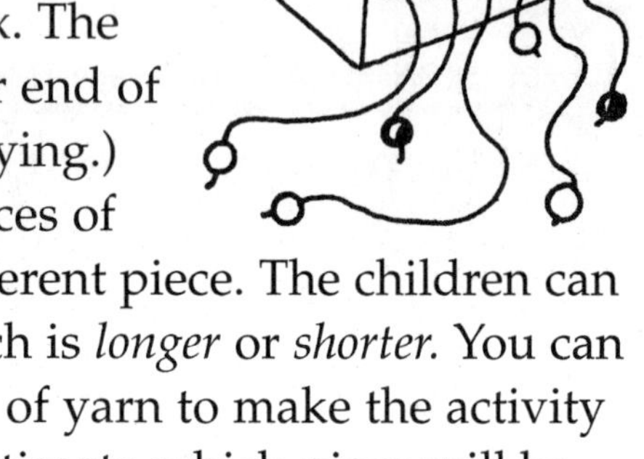

Prior to the activity, cut six small holes in one end of each shoebox. Place six different lengths of yarn into each shoebox. Ask the children to tie a bead on one end of each piece of yarn and thread the other end through a hole in the end of the shoebox. The children can then tie a bead on the other end of the yarn. (You may have to assist with tying.) One child pulls gently on one of the pieces of yarn, while another child pulls on a different piece. The children can compare their pieces of yarn to see which is *longer* or *shorter.* You can remove the beads and switch the pieces of yarn to make the activity different each time. Children can also estimate which piece will be the longest or shortest.

Literacy Center Ideas

Reading/Writing: The Inchworm

• **Materials:** paper, pencils, notecards

The children can write what might have happened to the inchworm after the end of the story. Prior to the unit, write the following prompts on notecards. *Where did the inchworm go? Did the inchworm measure more birds? Did the nightingale come to find the inchworm? What else did the inchworm measure?*

Math: Paper Clip Measure

• **Materials:** several paper clips per child

The children can use paper clips to measure the same items in the classroom as they did for the Application and Practice Activity. They can discuss why their answers were different this time and why.

Science: Balancing Buttons

- **Materials:** one ruler per child, one small cardboard tube for every two children, tape, two small paper cups per child, assorted buttons, paper, pencils, sample scale for the center, scissors

Prior to the activity, make a sample scale for the Math Center. The children will be making a *balance,* which is a type of *scale.* The children can cut each small cardboard tube in half lengthwise, share one half with a friend, and tape two paper cups to each end of a ruler. The children can balance the ruler on half of the cardboard tube to make a scale. Each child will take a handful of buttons to *weigh.* The children will discover which buttons weigh *more,* which weigh *less,* and which weigh the same. The children can record their answers on paper.

Art: Inch Poster

- **Materials:** one ruler per child, construction paper, scissors, glue

Prior to the lesson, model how to use a standard 12-inch ruler for the children and explain that they are going to make an Inch Poster. Everything on the poster will be one inch in *length.* Cut several pieces of construction paper into strips of different colors. The students will measure and cut the strips into one-inch pieces to use on their poster. They can create a design using their one-inch pieces.

Dramatic Play: Make-Believe Measuring

- **Materials:** several measuring cups, measuring spoons, bowls, and pans

The children can take turns pretending to measure ingredients while cooking something for one another in the dramatic play area. Encourage them to use the math vocabulary they are learning.

Kids in the Kitchen: Dirt Dessert

- **Materials:** one store-bought pudding cup per child, three gummy worms per child, one ruler per child, five chocolate cookies per child, one placemat per child

Caution: This activity uses edible items. Always check for food sensitivities and allergies before serving food or allowing children to handle food.

Each child should use a placemat for this activity. The children will each have three gummy worms and a ruler. They can measure their gummy worms and compare with a friend. *Whose worms are longer? Whose are shorter? Are the worms the same length?* To create their snack, the children will count out five chocolate cookies and crumble them in their pudding cup to resemble dirt. The children can add their gummy worms to their Dirt Dessert and enjoy.

Five Minute Math Fun: Longest/Shortest

- **Materials:** green and blue crayons, children's inchworm books

Ask the children to look in their inchworm books and circle the longest item with a green crayon and the shortest item with a blue crayon. They can compare their results with a partner.

Home Connection

Copy the Parent Letter on page 35 and send it home the week you are conducting this unit.

Date:

Dear Parents:

This week in math, we are working on measurement. We read the book *Inch by Inch* by Leo Lionni and talked about how the inchworm got away. We made inch posters, dirt dessert, and inchworm books. We also made our own scale and weighed buttons!

You can help your child learn more about measurement by helping him or her measure things around your home. Here are some suggestions:

- Start a growth chart for your child and measure him or her each month. Your child can share the results with the class.
- Compare the measurements of articles of clothing while sorting the laundry or putting away clothes. You might ask questions such as, "Which sock is longer? Which belt is shorter?"
- Show your child where you keep your tape measure or ruler and invite him or her to measure household items.

According to the National Council for Teachers of Mathematics, "Mathematics learning builds on the curiosity and enthusiasm of children and grows naturally from their experiences." It is important to give your child exposures to math in everyday life and let them explore.

Thank you for being an important part of your child's learning.

Sincerely,

Inchworm Patterns

London, Jonathan. (1992). *Froggy gets dressed.* New York: Penguin Books.

NCTM Standard: Data Analysis and Probability

"Through their data investigations, young students should develop the idea that data, charts, and graphs give information. When data are displayed in an organized manner, class discussions should focus on what the graph or other representation conveys and whether the data help answer the specific questions that were posed."

-NCTM Standards, 2000

In kindergarten through grade 2 all students should—

- pose questions and gather data about themselves and their surroundings.
- sort and classify objects according to their attributes and organize data about the objects.
- represent data using concrete objects, pictures, and graphs.
- describe parts of the data and the set of data as a whole to determine what the data show.
- discuss events related to students' experiences as likely or unlikely.

Math Vocabulary

record	conclusion	data	collect	organize
category	compare	classify	graph	how many

Prereading Activity

• **Materials:** *Froggy Gets Dressed* by Jonathan London

Read the title of the book with the children. Ask them to talk about the cover of the book and what they think the book will be about. Ask the children how looking at the cover can help them read the book.

Read-Aloud Activity

• **Materials:** *Froggy Gets Dressed* by Jonathan London

Read *Froggy Gets Dressed* with the children and invite them to join in the reading as the voice of Froggy when he says, "Wha-a-a-a-t?" Discuss and compare with the children what types of clothing they should wear to play outside in the winter and in the summer.

Application and Practice Activity

• **Materials:** Froggy's Clothes Chart, page 43, scissors, glue, magazines

Prior to the activity, copy one Froggy's Clothes Chart from page 43 for each child. The children can cut pictures from magazines and glue them in the appropriate *category* to complete the chart. Discuss with the children *how many* of each they found. Which category has more? Which category has less?

Extension Activity

• **Materials:** paper bag, colored counters, chart paper, markers

For this activity, you will need a paper bag full of different colored counters. Gather the children together and ask them to name the colors they see. Fold the bag closed and shake it. Ask a volunteer to pull out one counter and identify the color. Ask another volunteer

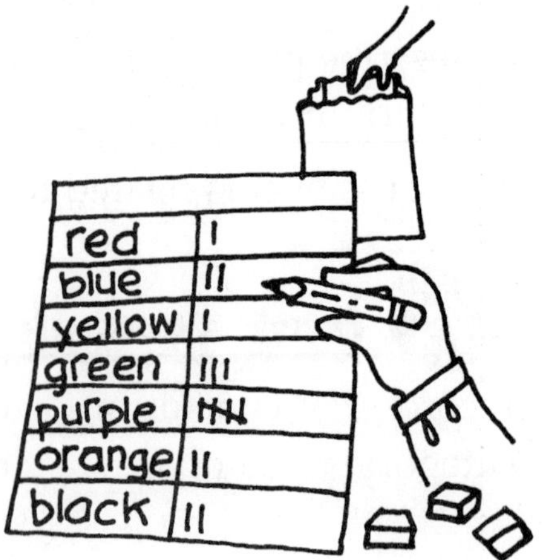

to *record* the color on chart paper. Repeat this five times with different students. Ask students to predict what will be the most probable color based upon these five pulls. Allow each child to pick one counter from the bag while one child continues to *record* the color on the chart. Stop after every fifth pull and make predictions based on the *data.* Repeat until all children have had an opportunity to draw a color. Help the children draw a *conclusion* to determine the most probable color. Discuss how the *data* was *collected* and *organized* on the chart.

Reading/Writing: Word Find

- **Materials:** note cards, pencils, two copies of *Froggy Gets Dressed* by Jonathan London, paper

Prior to the activity, write some of the high-frequency words from the story on several sets of note cards and put them in the Reading/Writing Center, along with at least two copies of the book. The children can reread the story and look for the high-frequency words. They can read and/or write the words.

Math: Frog Math Facts

- **Materials:** several pairs of dice, frog counters

Supply several pairs of dice and some frog counters in the math center. The children can roll the dice, add the two numbers together, and hop on one foot that many times. They can use the counters as manipulatives to help them with adding if needed. (If you do not have access to frog counters, others may be substituted.)

Science: Frog Watching

- **Materials:** aquarium, pond water, tadpoles, reference books, plastic magnifying glasses

Spring is the best time for this activity. Set up an aquarium in the classroom with water from a local pond. Bring in tadpoles for the children to observe. You can get them at a pet store, or conduct an online search using *tadpoles* as the key word. There are many books that provide photographic references to the life cycle of a frog. Display a few of these books in your classroom where students can match the photographs to what is happening in the aquarium. Children can discuss the stages of a frog's life.

Art: Froggy Doll

- **Materials:** Froggy paper doll and clothing patterns, pages 44–46, scissors, crayons, *Froggy Gets Dressed* by Jonathan London

Prior to the activity, copy the Froggy Paper Doll and Clothes patterns from pages 44–46 for each child and provide them in the art center. The children can color and cut them out. The children can retell the story and put the clothing on Froggy.

Dramatic Play: Dressing Like Froggy

- **Materials:** at least four each of the following clothing items: socks, boots, hats, scarves, mittens (you may want to ask parents for donations), numbered cubes or dice, chart

Prior to the activity, assign the numbers 1-6 to each item of clothing and make a picture chart showing which item goes with which number. The children can roll the die or cube and put on the corresponding item of clothing, as Froggy did in the story.

Kids in the Kitchen: Silly Snowmen

- **Materials:** round cookies, white frosting, licorice, chocolate chips, raisins, candy corn, gumdrops, plastic knives

***Caution:** This activity uses edible items. Always check for food sensitivities and allergies before serving food or allowing children to handle food.*

Children can use the materials to create a silly snowman. They can then *compare* their own with those of their classmates by asking questions such as, "How many buttons does your snowman have?" or "What kind of eyes does your snowman have?"

Five Minute Math Fun: I'm Dressed Like Froggy!

- **Materials:** chart paper, markers, *Froggy Gets Dressed* by Jonathan London

✓	✓	✓	✓	✓	✓	✓	✓
✓	✓	✓	✓	✓	✓	✓	✓
✓	✓		✓	✓	✓	✓	✓
✓	✓			✓	✓	✓	✓
✓	✓			✓	✓	✓	✓
✓				✓	✓	✓	✓
✓					✓	✓	✓
✓					✓	✓	✓
					✓	✓	✓
					✓	✓	✓
					✓	✓	

Create a *graph* based on the clothing items that Froggy was wearing in the story. The children can help fill in the data by placing a mark under the items that they wore to school that day. Explain that when you *classify* information, it is easier to understand.

Home Connection

Copy the Parent Letter on page 42 and send it home the week you are conducting this unit.

Date:

Dear Parents:

This week in math, we are working on data analysis and probability. We read the book *Froggy Gets Dressed* by Jonathan London and talked about gathering and recording data and probability. We hopped like frogs in our math center, watched tadpoles in our science center, and made silly snowmen for a snack!

You can help your child with data analysis and probability by taking advantage of learning opportunities that happen naturally during each day. Here are some suggestions:

- Help your child classify, sort, and organize at home when they are putting away toys, groceries, or laundry.
- Your child can reenact *Froggy Gets Dressed* at home with you.
- Make silly snowmen at home using round cookies, white frosting, licorice, chocolate chips, raisins, candy corn, and gumdrops. Ask your child to compare his or her snowman to yours.

The National Council for Teachers of Mathematics advises, "Children learn through exploring their world; thus, interests and everyday activities are natural vehicles for developing mathematical thinking."

The time you spend with your child is important. Thank you for your contributions.

Sincerely,

Froggy's Clothes Chart

Shoes	Coat
Pants	**Hat**

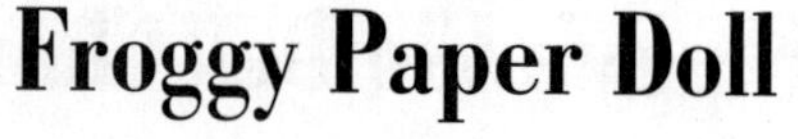

Froggy Paper Doll

Froggy Paper Doll Clothes

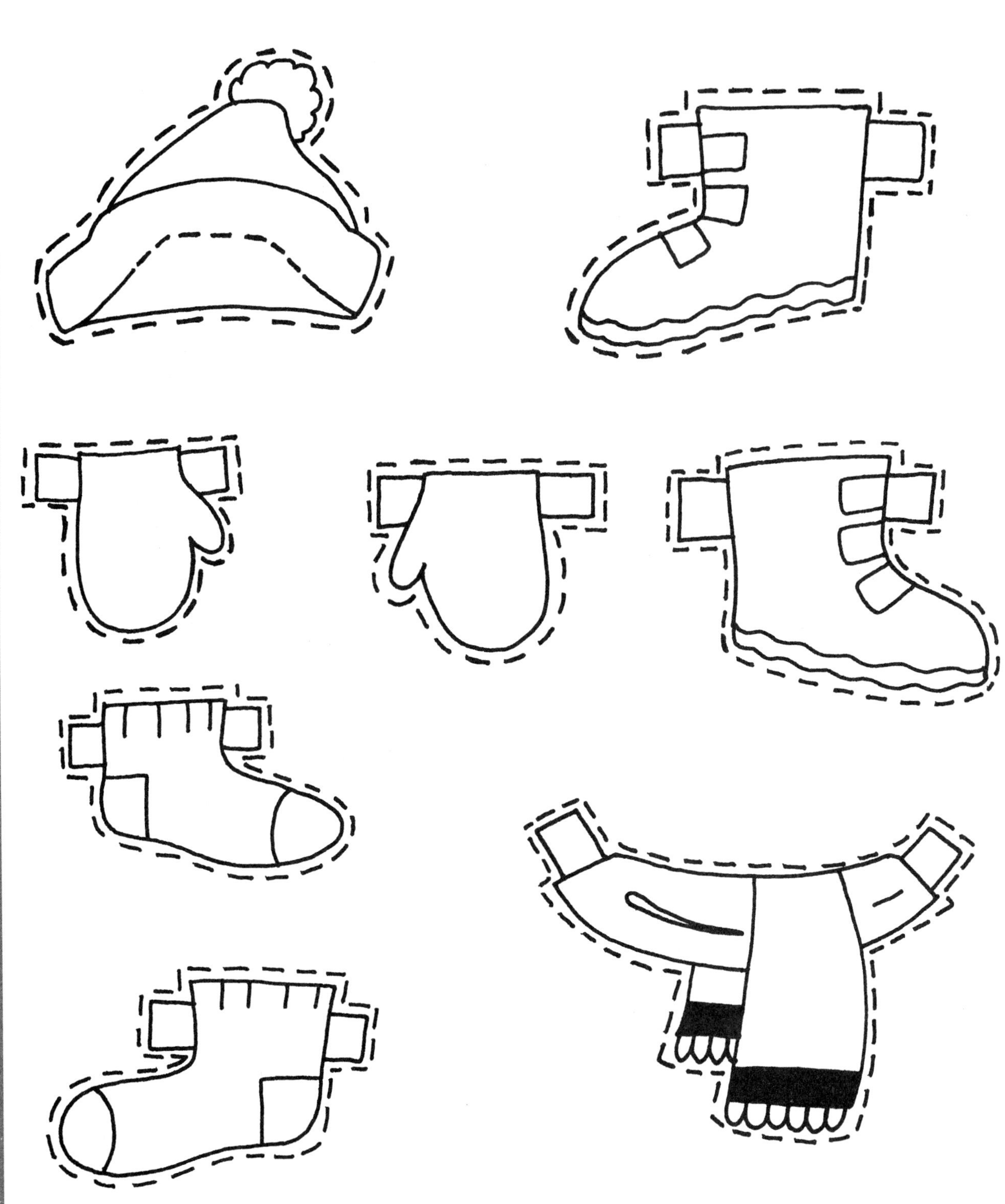

Froggy Paper Doll Clothes

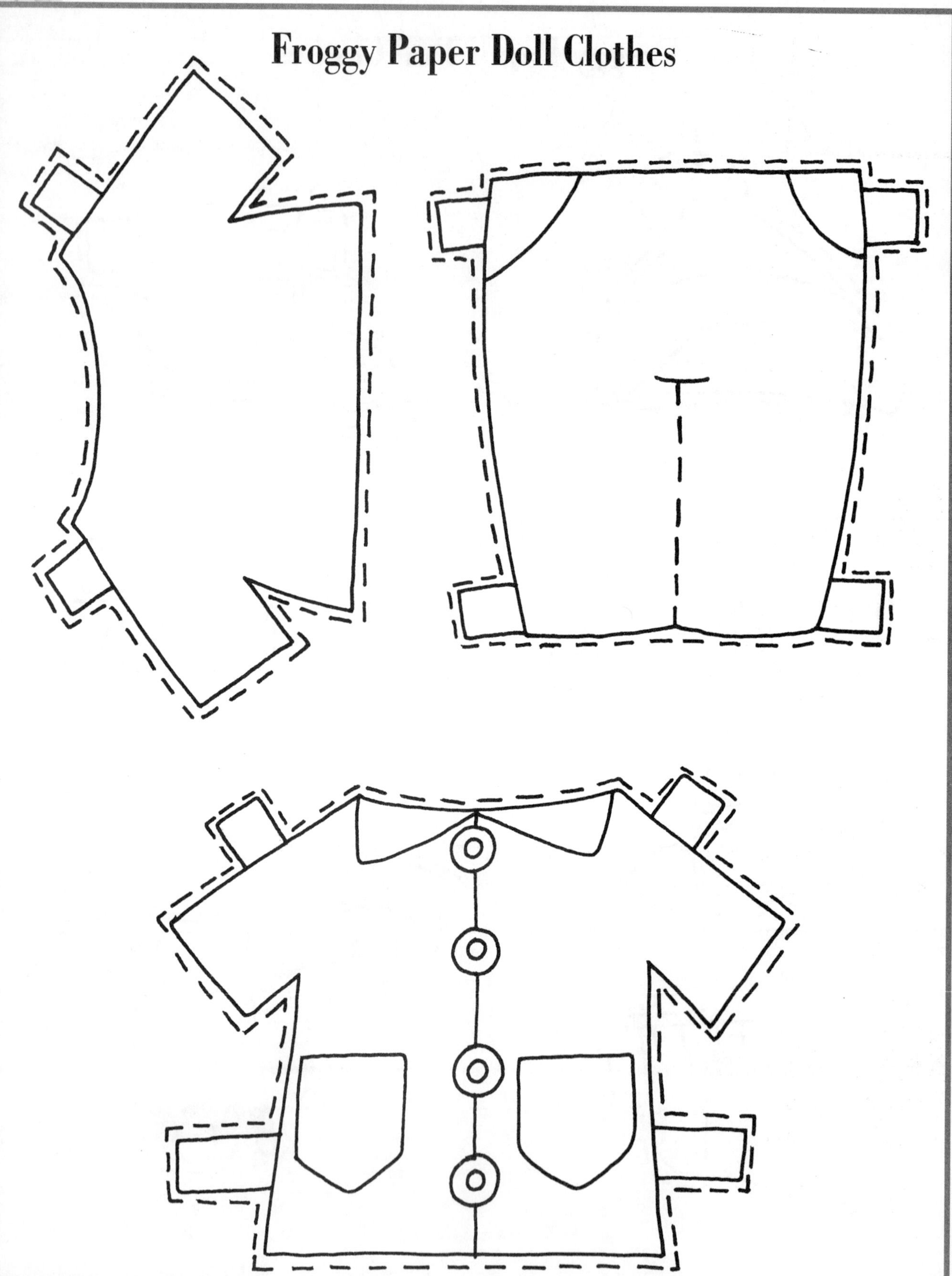

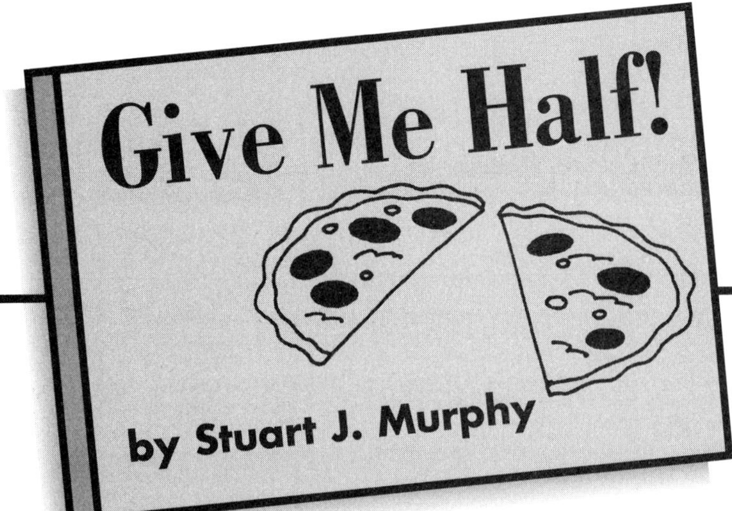

Murphy, Stuart J. (1996). ***Give me half!***
New York: Harper Collins.

NCTM Standard: Number and Operations

"Although fractions are not a topic for major emphasis for pre-k –2 students, informal experiences at this age will help develop a foundation for deeper learning in higher grades."

-NCTM Standards, 2000

In kindergarten through grade 2 all students should—

- count with understanding and recognize "how many" in sets of objects.
- connect number words and numerals to the quantities they represent, using various physical models and representations.
- understand and represent commonly used fractions, such as $\frac{1}{4}$, $\frac{1}{3}$, and $\frac{1}{2}$.

Math Vocabulary

fraction	half	part	measure	$\frac{1}{4}$	$\frac{1}{3}$	$\frac{1}{2}$
whole	equal	divide	share			

Prereading Activity

- **Materials:** *Give Me Half!* by Stuart J. Murphy, $\frac{1}{2}$, $\frac{1}{3}$, and $\frac{1}{4}$ measuring cups, a paper plate cut in half

Ask the children to read the title of the story with you. Ask them if they know what *half* means. Ask for a volunteer to demonstrate one *half* (such as one half of a piece of paper). Show the children the paper plate as a *whole,* then show them *half* of the paper plate, and explain that the *half* is *part* of the *whole.* Show the children the measuring cups and discuss how they are used. Ask the children if they have used measuring cups at home. Ask the children to tell you what they think this book will be about.

Read-Aloud Activity

- **Materials:** *Give Me Half!* by Stuart J. Murphy

Explain to the children that this book will be about sharing, and when you *share* or *divide* something with another person, you have created a *fraction*. Tell them that a *fraction* is *part* of a *whole* and that all of the parts together *equal* the whole.

As you read the story with the children, be sure that they notice the dog on each page. Discuss with the children what the dog is doing and how he might be feeling in each picture.

Application and Practice Activity

- **Materials:** two paper plates per child, crayons

The children can draw pictures of food items on their paper plates. They can draw the items from the story, or their favorite foods if they choose. Ask the children to use a black crayon and draw a line showing how they could *divide* the food fairly when sharing with another person.

Extension Activity

- **Materials:** 1, $\frac{1}{2}$, $\frac{1}{3}$, and $\frac{1}{4}$ measuring cups, 3-4 large plastic tubs, water, newspaper, food coloring

Cover the floor in the work area with newspaper prior to this activity. Partially fill each tub with water. Ask the children to help you decide which colors to put in the water. Allow the children to explore using the measuring cups and water. Explain that they can *measure* the water in the smaller cups to find out how many of them will fill the larger cups. Write the fractions $\frac{1}{4}$, $\frac{1}{3}$, and $\frac{1}{2}$ on the chalkboard and ask the children to find the corresponding measuring cups.

Literacy Center Ideas

Reading/Writing: Share and Share Alike

- **Materials:** paper, pencils, crayons

The children can write and/or draw about a time when they didn't want to share something. They can tell what it was and why they didn't want to share.

Math: Fraction Fun

- **Materials:** tangrams, fraction circles, base ten blocks, paper plates cut in halves, thirds, and fourths, paper napkins, notecards, markers

Prior to the activity, make some fraction notecards by writing the fraction on one side and drawing several fraction pictures on the other side. The children can explore fractions in the Math Center. Using the provided materials, they will be able to put pieces together and take them apart to make visual fractions. The children can use the fraction notecards if needed.

Science: Measuring Cup Fractions

- **Materials:** sensory table, several 1, $\frac{1}{2}$, $\frac{1}{3}$, and $\frac{1}{4}$ measuring cups, rice, cotton balls, and sand in containers for the sensory table

The children can use the rice, cotton balls, or sand in the sensory table to fill the measuring cups. They can use the smaller cups to see how many of them will fill a larger cup. The children can compare how many cotton balls will fill each cup with how much sand or rice will fill each cup. The children can share the results with one another.

Art: Fraction Art

- **Materials:** several construction paper circles in different colors and sizes cut into halves, thirds, and fourths, glue, one 9"x12" piece of white construction paper per child

The children can use the fraction pieces to construct pictures and glue them to the 9"x12" piece of paper.

Dramatic Play: Friend Fractions

- **Materials:** large roll of paper, crayons

The children can use their bodies to help each other make fractions. For example, they can each put one hand down and then divide them in half. They can also stand next to two or three friends to show $\frac{1}{3}$ or $\frac{1}{4}$. The children can trace each other on paper and use their crayons to decorate and divide the body in half.

Kids in the Kitchen: $\frac{1}{2}$ and $\frac{1}{2}$ Sandwich

- **Materials:** one whole graham cracker per child, peanut butter, one large marshmallow per child, one chocolate bar per child, plastic knives, one piece of waxed paper per child, one small plastic bag per child (You may want to ask parents to donate these items.)

Caution: ***This activity uses edible items. Always check for food sensitivities and allergies before serving food or allowing children to handle food.***

Each child should make their snack on a piece of waxed paper. The children can use a plastic knife to cut the graham cracker, marshmallow, and chocolate bar in *half*. They can also use the plastic knife to spread peanut butter on *half* of the graham cracker. To make their sandwich, the children can layer *half* of the chocolate bar and *half* of the marshmallow on each *half* of the graham cracker. The children can eat *half* of their snack and put the other *half* in a plastic bag to take home.

Five Minute Math Fun: Color the Fractions

- **Materials:** Color the Fractions activity, page 53, crayons or markers

Copy the Color the Fractions activity on page 53 for each child and distribute. The children can color one half of each picture.

Home Connection

Copy the Parent Letter on page 52 and send it home the week you are conducting this unit.

Date:

Dear Parents:

This week in math we are working on number and operations. We read *Give Me Half!* by Stuart J. Murphy and talked about understanding basic fractions, dividing in half, and sharing. We made $\frac{1}{2}$ and $\frac{1}{2}$ sandwiches as a snack, measured with sand, cotton, and rice in our sensory table, and made fractions with our friends.

You can help your child learn more about fractions by involving him or her in everyday tasks at home. Here are some suggestions:

- Invite your child to help you when you are cooking or baking something. He or she can help measure the ingredients.
- When you are cutting a pizza, a cake, or a pie into pieces at home, discuss the fractions you are making with your child.
- When you serve food to your child, ask him or her how it could be divided in half to share with someone.

The National Council for Teachers of Mathematics reminds, "Children need introductions to the language and conventions of mathematics, at the same time maintaining a connection to their informal knowledge and language. They should hear mathematical language being used in meaningful contexts."

Children will begin to develop positive attitudes toward math when parents share some fun math-related activities. Thank you for your participation.

Sincerely,

Color the Fractions

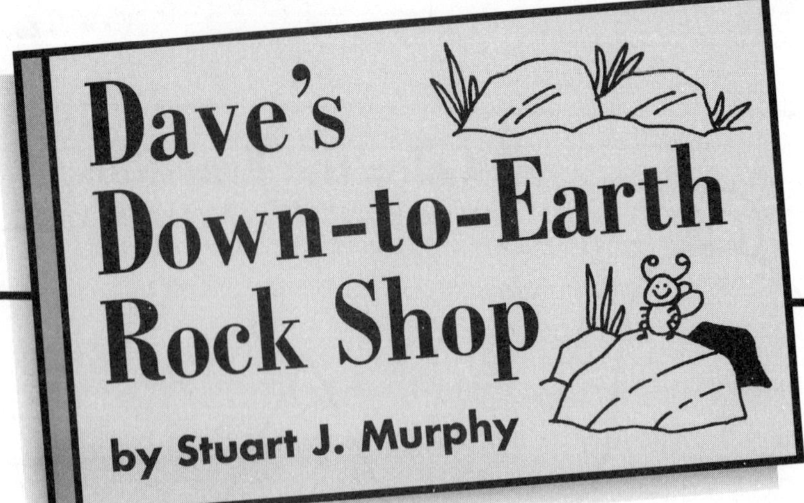

Murphy, Stuart J. (2000). *Dave's down-to-earth rock shop.* New York: Harper Collins.

NCTM Standard: Data Analysis and Probability

"Informal comparing, classifying, and counting activities can provide the mathematical beginnings for developing young learners' understanding of data, analysis of data, and statistics."

-NCTM Standards, 2000

In prekindergarten through grade 2 all students should—

- pose questions and gather data about themselves and their surroundings.
- sort and classify objects according to their attributes and organize data about the objects.
- represent data using concrete objects, pictures, and graphs.
- describe parts of the data and the set of data as a whole to determine what the data show.

Math Vocabulary

sort	classify	organize	gather	attribute
color	shape	size	collection	group

Prereading Activity

- **Materials:** *Dave's Down-to-Earth Rock Shop* by Stuart J. Murphy, several rocks in various sizes, shapes, and colors

Read the title with the children. Ask the children if any of them have ever had a *collection* of something, like rocks. Talk about sorting collections. Discuss and explain what an *attribute* is and give examples, such as *color, size,* and *shape*. Use the rocks to illustrate the examples. Explain to the children that a *geologist* is someone who studies rocks.

Read-Aloud Activity

- **Materials:** *Dave's Down-to-Earth Rock Shop* by Stuart J. Murphy, several rocks in various sizes, shapes, and colors

Read the book aloud with the children. Discuss why Josh and Amy wanted to *gather* more rocks for their collection. Ask the children to help you *sort, classify,* and *organize* the rocks you brought. Each *group* of rocks will have a different *attribute*.

Application and Practice Activity

- **Materials:** two paper bags, several pairs of items that are easily identified by touch (crayons, paper clips, sponges)

Divide the items equally into each bag. Give each child an object from the first bag. Ask the children to describe the attributes of the item. Pass around the second bag and ask the children to feel inside and find an item that is similar to the first object. When all have chosen a second object, ask the children to describe how the attributes of the second item are similar or different from the first.

Extension Activity

- **Materials:** several items from the classroom environment, such as books, toys, pencils, and so on

Place the collected items in the middle of the room and ask the children to form a circle around them. Each child can take a turn to pick three items that have at least one attribute in common. For example, a ruler, a clock, and a scale all have numbers. The child can share the common attribute with class. Continue until all children have had a turn.

Reading/Writing: Name Sort

- **Materials:** paper, pencils, sentence strips

Prior to the activity, print each child's first name on a sentence strip. Make these strips available in the Reading/Writing Center. The children can sort the names according to the number of letters, the beginning letter, and so on. They can make a chart or list to show their findings.

Math: Rock Candy Math

- **Materials:** store-bought rock candy in various colors, 3-4 simple scales, rulers

Caution: *This activity uses edible items. Always check for food sensitivities and allergies before serving food or allowing children to handle food.*

The children can use the scale and ruler to measure the rock candy and sort it according to size, shape, weight, color, and finally, taste.

Science: Interesting Inspections

- **Materials:** 4–5 plastic magnifying glasses, various kinds of leaves, seeds, and rocks

The children can use the magnifying glass to inspect each leaf, seed, and rock and classify them according to attributes such as type, size, shape, or color.

Art: Rolling Rocks

- **Materials:** several shallow box lids, paper, various small rounded rocks, different colors of tempera paint in cups, newspaper, paintbrushes

Prior to the lesson, cover the work area with newspapers. The children can put a piece of paper in the box lid. They can use a paintbrush to paint a rock and put it in the box lid. By tilting the box lid, the children can gently roll the rock around to paint their paper. The children can use a different rock for each color.

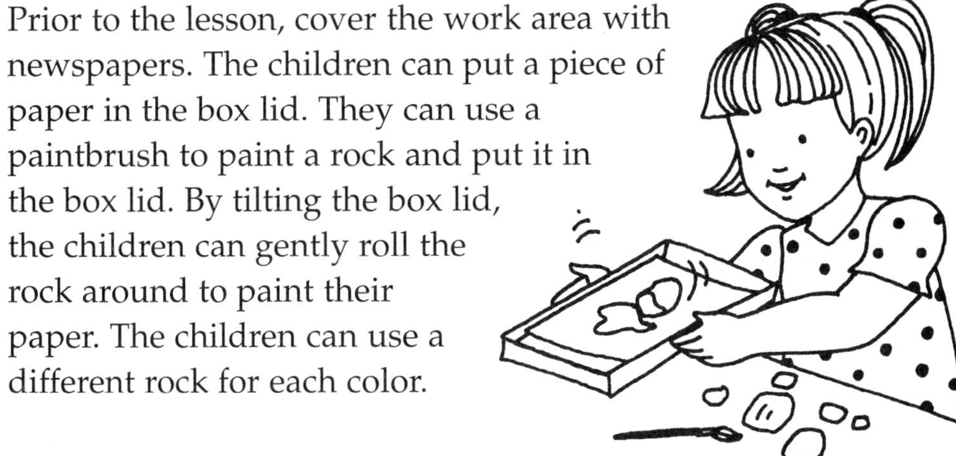

Dramatic Play: Future Geologists

- **Materials:** sensory table, various rocks, sand or dirt, small plastic shovels, small paintbrushes

Prior to the activity, put the rocks and dirt or sand in the sensory table along with the tools. The children can pretend to be geologists. They can use the tools to dig for and uncover the rocks in the sensory table.

Kids in the Kitchen: Munchie Mix

- **Materials:** one paper or plastic bowl per child, several small nut cups per child, a large bowl, a large spoon, miniature marshmallows, several different kinds of cereal pieces, chocolate candies, and any other snack food you would like to include

Prior to the activity, combine all of the ingredients in a large bowl. The children can use the spoon to put a serving of the mix in their bowls. Then they can sort and classify their munchies in nut cups according to the attributes. (For example, size, shape, or color.) The children will enjoy munching on their Munchie Mix!

***Caution:** This activity uses edible items. Always check for food sensitivities and allergies before serving food or allowing children to handle food.*

Five Minute Math Fun: Rock Boxes

- **Materials:** several shoe boxes with a hole cut in one end, various kinds of rocks to go inside the box

Place several rocks inside the boxes. The children can reach in the box, feel the rocks, and describe the attributes of the rocks. Allow each child to have a turn.

Home Connection

Copy the Parent Letter on page 59 and send it home the week you are conducting this unit.

Date:

Dear Parents:

This week in math, we are working on classifying and sorting objects according to their attributes. We read the book *Dave's Down-to-Earth Rock Shop* by Stuart J. Murphy and talked about collections. We painted pictures using rolling rocks, measured and sorted rock candy, and inspected leaves, seeds, and rocks in our sensory table.

You can help your child learn more about classifying and sorting by involving them in related activities at home. Here are some suggestions:

- Ask your child to sort his or her toys according to a particular attribute.
- Take your child to the grocery store and help him or her classify the groceries in the cart according to what section they belong to in the store.
- While putting away groceries, laundry, or toys, ask your child to pick three objects and describe one attribute that the objects have in common.

Carol Sue Fromboluti and Natalie Rinck, early childhood experts, remind us, "Some children may need extra guidance when doing some activities. The younger the child, the more important it is to keep the activities short and focus on the activities that use objects your child can touch and play with."

When you turn everyday events into teachable moments, the impact is very powerful. Thank you for your cooperation.

Sincerely,

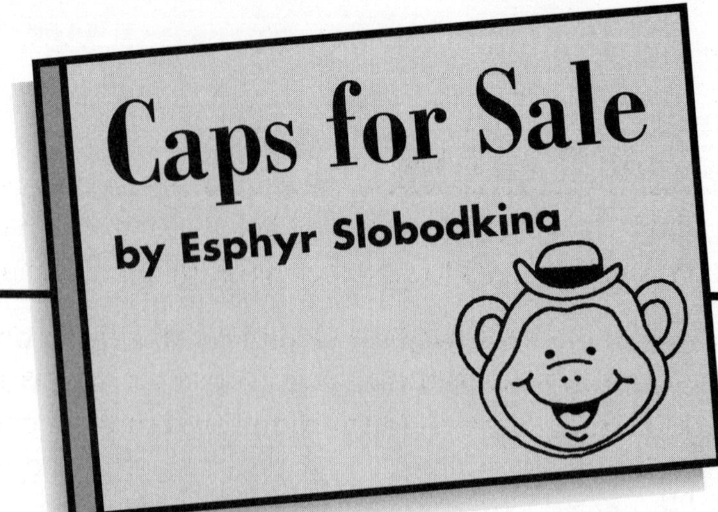

Slobodkina, Esphyr. (1987). *Caps for sale.* New York: Scholastic.

NCTM Standard: Problem Solving

"Problem solving in the early years should involve a variety of contexts, from problems related to daily routines to mathematical situations arising from stories."

-NCTM Standards, 2000

Instructional programs from prekindergarten through grade 2 should enable students to—

- build new mathematical knowledge through problem solving.
- solve problems that arise in mathematics and in other contexts.
- apply and adapt a variety of appropriate strategies to solve problems.
- monitor and reflect on the process of mathematical problem solving.

Math Vocabulary

sort	organize	count	problem solve	observe
predict	estimate	compare	guess	

Prereading Activity

- **Materials:** *Caps for Sale* by Esphyr Slobodkina, one hat per child (You may ask parents to send one with their child that day.)

Ask the children to put on their hats and read the title of the story with you. Read the subtitle to them and discuss the words *peddler* and *monkey business*. Ask the children if they can find the monkeys hiding on the cover.

Read-Aloud Activity

- **Materials:** *Caps for Sale* by Esphyr Slobodkina

Read *Caps for Sale* with the children. Ask them to join in when the peddler says his repetitive line. Discuss the word *wares*. On the page that shows the peddler waking up from his nap, stop and ask the children what they *observe*. (His caps are gone.) Continue reading and stop on the page that shows the peddler looking up into the tree. Ask the children to *predict* what the peddler saw. On the page that shows the monkeys in the tree, stop and ask the children to *count* the monkeys. Ask how many caps there are. Discuss with the children that if each monkey is wearing a cap, there must be the same number of caps.

Application and Practice Activity

- **Materials:** magazines, scissors, chart paper, glue

The children can find and cut out pictures of different kinds of hats from magazines. Discuss with the children the different types of hats, who might wear them, and why. Ask the children to *sort* out the hats and *organize* them according to size or color. Make a chart and ask the children to graph the types of hats they found.

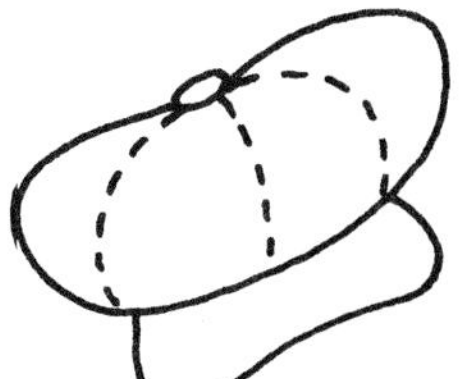

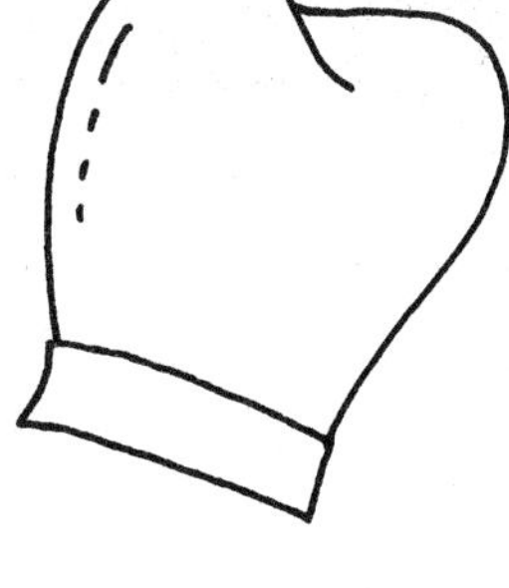

Extension Activity

- **Materials:** 3-4 interlocking monkey games

To help them *problem solve,* the children can play an interlocking monkey game. They can empty the monkeys on the table and pick up one monkey by an arm. Next, they try to hook another monkey through the other arm. The children can continue to make a chain. Their turn is over when a monkey drops from the chain. For added fun, ask the children to balance 2 or more hats on their head during their turn.

Reading/Writing: What Would You Sell?

- **Materials:** paper, pencils, two $8\frac{1}{2}$" x 11" pieces of paper per child

Prior to the activity, write *Caps! Caps for sale! Fifty cents a cap!* on an $8\frac{1}{2}$" x 11" piece of paper for each child to use as a model. The children should think about what kinds of wares they would sell if they were a peddler. They can make their own sign for what they would sell and how much it would cost, and draw a picture of it.

Math: Monkey Math

- **Materials:** Monkey Counters Pattern, page 67, Tree Pattern, page 66, one spinner for each pair of children

Copy the Monkey Counters and Tree Pattern pages for each child. The children can cut out the monkeys and color them if they wish. Working with a partner, one child can spin the spinner and put that many monkeys in the tree. The other child then spins the spinner and either adds that many monkeys to the tree or takes that many monkeys out of the tree. Both children can count the final number of monkeys together.

Science: Taste Test

- **Materials:** several different types of fruit for sampling, (cut into bite-sized pieces) such as bananas, nectarines, kiwi, and so on, one plastic spoon, one paper plate, and one blindfold per child

<u>Caution:</u> This activity uses edible items. Always check for food sensitivities and allergies before serving food or allowing children to handle food.

The children can put on a blindfold and taste different kinds of fruit. They can *guess* the fruit and take off the blindfold to check their guess.

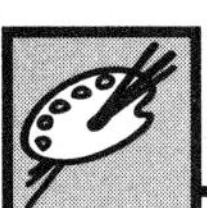

Art: Creating Caps

- **Materials:** one white painter's cap per child, fabric markers (These can be obtained at hobby stores, or you may want to ask parents for donations.)

The children can use the fabric markers to decorate their own cap and imitate the monkeys in the story.

Dramatic Play: Monkey See, Monkey Do

- **Materials:** full-length mirrors, hand-held mirrors

The children can get an idea of what imitation looks like by using a full-length or hand-held mirror and making faces or movements while looking in the mirror. The children can also stand facing a partner and try to imitate their partner's actions or facial expressions.

Kids in the Kitchen: Monkey Mix Estimation

- **Materials:** dried banana chips, pretzels, chocolate chips, various types of cereal, one paper bowl and one plastic bag per child, paper, pencils

Caution: ***This activity uses edible items. Always check for food sensitivities and allergies before serving food or allowing children to handle food.***

Prior to this activity, place a random amount of each ingredient into a plastic bag for each child. The children can *estimate* and write down how many ingredients they think are in their bag. They can then *count* the items and place them in their bowl as they count. After counting, the children can *compare* their estimates to the actual answers and enjoy the snack!

Five Minute Math Fun: How Much Money?

- **Materials:** 32 pretend plastic quarters, *Caps for Sale* by Esphyr Slobodkina

Ask the children to guess how much money the peddler would make if he sold all of his caps. The children can count the number of caps he has for sale and count out fifty cents per cap. Explain that fifty cents plus fifty cents equals one dollar and help the children total the amount.

Home Connection

Copy the Parent Letter on page 65 and send it home the week you are conducting this unit.

Date:

Dear Parents:

This week in math, we are working on problem solving. We read the book *Caps for Sale* by Esphyr Slobodkina and talked about sorting, organizing, and estimating. We made Monkey Mix, played Monkey See, Monkey Do, and created caps to wear.

You can help your child with problem solving by allowing him or her to help figure out solutions to simple problems in everyday life. Here are some suggestions:

- If your child receives an allowance, give it to him or her in a different denomination and count it together.
- Play games with your child that involve problem solving, such as mystery games, guessing games, and estimating games.
- Encourage your child to suggest problems and ask questions. Your child will learn how to figure things out and that many problems can be solved several different ways.

Early childhood experts Carol Sue Fromboluti and Natalie Rinck suggest, "Problem solving is key in being able to do all other aspects of mathematics. Through problem solving, children learn that there are many different ways to solve a problem and that more than one answer is possible."

Encouraging your child to figure things out will help him or her solve problems with ease. Thank you for your participation.

Sincerely,

Tree Pattern

Monkey Counters

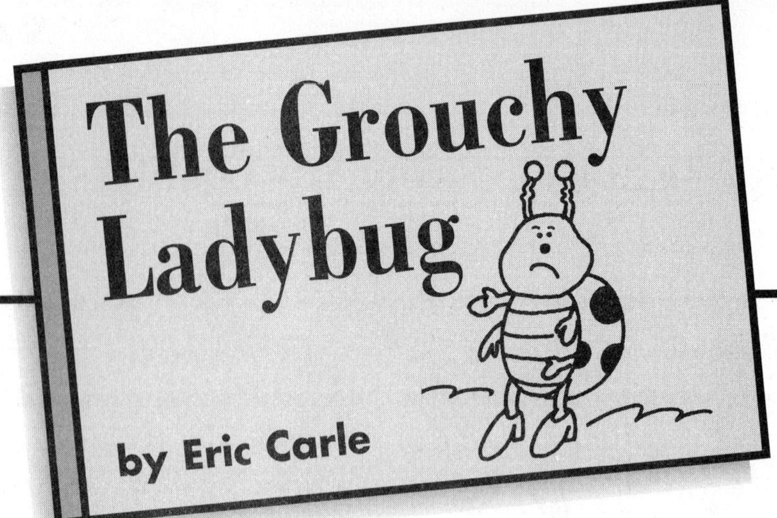

Carle, Eric. (1977). *The grouchy ladybug.* New York: Harper Collins.

NCTM Standard: Measurement

"When students use calendars or sequence events in stories, they are using measures of time in a real context. Opportunities arise throughout the school day for teachers to focus on time and its measurement through short conversations with their students."

-NCTM Standards, 2000

In kindergarten through grade 2 all students should—

- recognize the attributes of length, volume, weight, area, and time.
- compare and order objects according to these attributes.
- select an appropriate unit and tool for the attribute being measured.
- develop common referents for measures to make comparisons and estimates.

Math Vocabulary

clock hour minute telling time o'clock

Prereading Activity

- **Materials:** *The Grouchy Ladybug* by Eric Carle, a large prop clock

Read the title of the book with the children. Ask them to tell you what *grouchy* means. Ask the children why they think the ladybug is grouchy. Hold up the clock and explain to the children that there will be a *clock* on almost every page of this book, and that they will be learning about *telling time*. Ask the children why they think it is important to know how to tell time.

Read-Aloud Activity

- **Materials:** *The Grouchy Ladybug* by Eric Carle, a large demonstration clock, one small demonstration clock per child

Give a brief explanation/demonstration of the longer and shorter hands of a clock and where they are located. Ask the children if anyone knows how to tell time. Those children that know can help you explain to their classmates about telling time on the *hour.* Point to, label, and count the *minute* dividers on the clock with the children. Model and discuss one o'clock, two o'clock, and so on.

Read the story aloud with the children. Ask them to watch for the clock on each page. Stop at each page and set your demonstration clock to the same time as the clock in the book. The children can use the clock in the book or your clock as a model to make their clock reflect the same time.

Application and Practice Activity

- **Materials:** Clock Pattern, page 75, one paper plate per child, one paper fastener per child, scissors, crayons, glue, pictures of daily activities, such as eating, sleeping, and so on

Prior to the activity, copy the Clock Pattern from page 75 for each child. The children can color and cut out the clock and hands and fasten them together with a paper fastener. Then the children can glue the clock to the paper plate. Assist if necessary.

Discuss different times of the day and ask the children what they are usually doing during those times. Display a picture of an activity and ask the children to name the activity. The children can then set their clock to the time that he or she would be doing that activity during the day. Assist when necessary.

Write the number and word forms of the time on a dry erase board, and explain that time can be written in both of these ways. For example: six *o'clock* or 6:00.

Extension Activity

- **Materials:** 12 large index cards, markers, 12 tagboard squares

Write times to the hour between 1:00 and 12:00 on each index card, and a number between 1 and 12 on each tagboard square. Place the tagboard squares faceup in a large circle to form a clock face.

Ask the children to sit around the clock. Give 12 children each an index card to keep facedown. Ask two volunteers, one taller than the other, to stand in the center of the clock.

Ask the children questions such as:

- "Who should be the minute hand and why?"
  (The taller child should be the minute hand, because the minute hand is longer.)
- "Where should the taller child point to show 1 o'clock?"
  (The taller child should point to the number 12.)
- "Where should the shorter child point to show 1 o'clock?"
  (The shorter child should point to the number 1.)

The children will take turns holding up their index cards while the volunteers point to the appropriate number. Repeat the activity until all of the children have had a turn.

Literacy Center Ideas

Reading/Writing: TV Time

- **Materials:** several television guides, paper, pencils, 3-4 small demonstration clocks

The children can look in the television guides for their favorite television shows and write down the name of the shows and what time they are shown on television. The children can also practice telling time using their demonstration clocks to show the time for a particular show.

Math: Ladybugs Landing

- **Materials:** 6-8 ladybug beanbag toys (ask parents to loan these to the class), a piece of cardboard painted green and cut into a large leaf shape (see picture)

The children can stand apart from the leaf and toss the ladybug beanbags. They can count the spots on all of the ladybugs that are touching the leaf for their score.

Science: Ladybug Inn

- **Materials:** one clear plastic deli container with lid per child, raisins, plastic knives, paper towels, twigs, grass, magnifying glasses

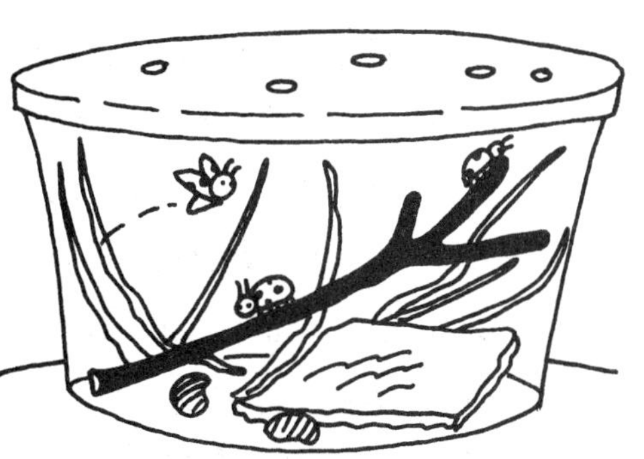

Wash out and dry the clear plastic deli containers and poke a few holes in the lids prior to the unit. The children can soak some raisins in water for a few minutes, cut them in half with the plastic knife, and place them on the bottom of the container. For a water supply, the children can wet a paper towel, squeeze it out, and fold it into a small square. They can add a few twigs or some grass for a crawling surface. The children have now created the Ladybug Inn!

When the children go outside to play, they can scout out some ladybug guests on garden plants, weeds or shrubs and gently brush them into the inn. You can also order ladybugs online by conducting a search. The children can use a magnifying glass to get a close-up view of their ladybug friends. In a day or two, the children can release their guests outside where they found them.

Art: Ladybug Thumbprints

- **Materials:** white construction paper, red and black tempera paint, wet sponges, newspaper, paper plates

Cover the work area with newspaper prior to the project. Pour a small amount of red and black paint on two separate plates. The children can use their thumb to dip in the red paint and make a thumbprint for the ladybug's body. The children can then use their pinky finger to dip in the black paint and make spots and a head for their ladybug. They can use the sponge to wipe their fingers clean.

Dramatic Play: Let's Pretend

- **Materials:** *The Grouchy Ladybug* by Eric Carle, several small demonstration clocks

The children can reenact the story by role playing the different characters from the book and putting the same time on their clocks to match the time of day in the book.

Kids in the Kitchen: Ladybug Clock Snack

- **Materials:** placemats, one round pre-made waffle per child, red frosting, miniature chocolate chips, black licorice, plastic knives, *The Grouchy Ladybug* by Eric Carle

***Caution:* The activity uses edible items. Always check for food sensitivities and allergies before serving food or allowing children to handle food.**

The children can use a plastic knife to spread red frosting on the waffle. The children can then use the miniature chocolate chips as the minute markers on the clock and the black licorice as the hands. They can find their favorite page in the book and put that time of day on their clock snack.

Five Minute Math Fun: What Time Is It?

- **Materials:** What Time Is It? activity, page 76, pencils, one small demonstration clock per child

Prior to the activity, copy one activity page per child. The children can write the time on each clock, either in number or word form. The children can also use a demonstration clock to help them if needed.

Home Connection

Copy the Parent Letter on page 74 and send it home the week you are conducting this unit.

Date:

Dear Parents:

This week in math, we are working on telling time. We read the book *The Grouchy Ladybug* by Eric Carle and talked about hours, minutes, and how to use a clock. We made our own clock from a paper plate, played a math game called Ladybugs Landing, and made a Ladybug Inn to bring home.

You can help your child learn more about telling time by incorporating activities and vocabulary related to time into everyday routines. Here are some suggestions:

- Use words such as hours, minutes, days, months, and years when talking with your child in relation to time. Try to avoid phrases such as "in a little while" which can be difficult to measure.

- Try setting time limits for routine activities, such as reading books or brushing teeth. This will help your child gain a better understanding of the concept of time.

- Ask your child to predict how long it will take him or her to perform a particular task, such as put their toys away. You can time the activity and compare the actual time with the prediction.

The National Council for Teachers of Mathematics indicates, "Because young children develop a disposition for mathematics from their early experiences, opportunities for learning should be positive and supportive. Children must learn to trust their own abilities to make sense of mathematics."

Thank you for contributing to your child's mathematical understanding.

Sincerely,

Clock Pattern

What Time Is It?

Harris, Trudy. (2000). *Pattern fish.* Connecticut: Millbrook Press.

NCTM Standard: Reasoning and Proof/Connections

"Two important elements of reasoning for students in the early grades are pattern recognition and classification skills. Creating and describing patterns offer important opportunities for students to make conjectures and give reasons for their validity."

-NCTM Standards, 2000

Instructional programs from prekindergarten through grade 2 should enable all students to—

- recognize reasoning and proof as fundamental aspects of mathematics.
- make and investigate mathematical conjectures.
- develop and evaluate mathematical arguments and proofs.
- select and use various types of reasoning and methods of proof.

Math Vocabulary

pattern observation design repeat

Prereading Activity

- **Materials:** *Pattern Fish* by Trudy Harris

Read the title of the book with the children. Ask the children to look around the room to see if they can make an *observation* to find a *pattern*. Ask them what a pattern looks like and discuss different types of patterns, such as "A-B-A-B" or "red-white-red-white." Explain to the children that a pattern is a *design* that *repeats*, and this book is about patterns and different kinds of fish.

Read-Aloud Activity

- **Materials:** *Pattern Fish* by Trudy Harris

Read the book aloud with the children. Ask them to complete the pattern on each page; for example, when you read the page with the yellow and black fish, the children should say "black" to complete the pattern. Be sure to read the explanation of patterns in the back of the book with the children.

Application and Practice Activity

- **Materials:** *Pattern Fish* by Trudy Harris

Ask the children to play the following characters in the story: the fish, eel, sea horse, puffer fish, octopus, jellyfish, and shark. They can act out the parts as you reread the story. At the end when the shark arrives, they can scurry away while recreating the pattern and performing the action of the fish!

Extension Activity

- **Materials:** *Pattern Fish* by Trudy Harris

Reread the story with the children and use alphabet letters to represent the patterns. For example, the first pattern is an A-B pattern; the second is an A-B-B pattern, and so on. This will help the children identify patterns more easily.

Literacy Center Ideas

Reading/Writing: Sea Life Search

- **Materials:** several copies of *Pattern Fish* by Trudy Harris, paper, pencils, crayons

The children can look through the book to find other examples of marine life (snail, starfish, frog, turtle, worm) and write them down on paper. They can decide what action or noise that the marine animal would make, create a pattern, and write it down. The children can also illustrate their marine animals.

Math: Perfect Patterns

- **Materials:** *Pattern Fish* by Trudy Harris, pattern blocks, linking cubes, buttons, tiles

The children can use the math manipulatives to recreate the patterns on each page from the book and to make their own patterns if they choose.

Science: Aquarium in a Bag

- **Materials:** clear hair gel, one plastic zipper bag per child, blue food coloring, gummy fish or fish stickers, newspaper

Put newspaper on the table and floor prior to the activity. The children can squeeze some hair gel and a few drops of blue food coloring into the plastic bag, add some fish, and seal it. As they "squish" the aquarium with their hands, they can see the fish wiggle around and feel the texture of the gel through the bag.

Art: Bubble Wrap Fish Prints

- **Materials:** several small pieces of bubble wrap, Bubble Wrap Fish Pattern, page 83, various colors of tempera paint, paper plates, newspaper

Copy one fish pattern from page 83 for each child. Prior to the activity, cover the work area with newspaper and put a small amount of paint on each paper plate. The children can dip the bubble wrap in the paint and make bubble wrap prints on the fish for scales.

Dramatic Play: Pretend Pond

- **Materials:** stuffed or inflatable marine animals, large inflatable pool, swimming goggles, shovels, buckets, dowels with yarn tied to one end, small toy boats

Inflate the pool prior to the activity. The children can use the materials to create a pretend pond in the classroom. They can pretend to be fish or other marine animals and reenact the story if they choose.

Kids in the Kitchen: Fishing for a Snack

- **Materials:** one pretzel rod per child, one gummy worm per child, one thin licorice rope per child, plastic knives, peanut butter, several fish crackers in a small cup for each child

<u>Caution:</u> This activity uses edible items. Always check for food sensitivities and allergies before serving food or allowing children to handle food.

The children can tie one end of the licorice around the pretzel and tie the gummy worm to the other end. They can use the plastic knife to spread peanut butter on the worm and dip it into a cup full of fish crackers to go "fishing for a snack."

Five Minute Math Fun: Pattern Parade

- **Materials:** none needed

This activity works best in good weather. Take the children on a short outdoor walk in search of patterns in the environment. Discuss the patterns in terms of alphabet letters as well (for example, A–B–A–B) to remind the children that patterns can be labeled in different ways.

Home Connection

Copy the Parent Letter on page 82 and send it home the week you are conducting this unit.

Date:

Dear Parents:

This week in math, we are working on pattern recognition. We read the book *Pattern Fish* by Trudy Harris and talked about patterns, designs, and making observations. We made bubble wrap fish prints, went fishing for a snack, and made an aquarium in a bag!

You can help your child with pattern recognition by calling his or her attention to simple patterns in the everyday environment. Here are some suggestions:

- Help your child find patterns in designs and pictures in your home or in a restaurant.
- String pasta or cereal into a simple pattern with your child. Challenge your child by increasing the difficulty of the pattern as needed.
- Use household items such as buttons or keys to create patterns with your child.

According to early childhood experts Carol Sue Fromboluti and Natalie Rinck, "Patterns...are important because they help us understand the underlying structure of things; they help us feel confident and capable of knowing what will come next, even when we can't see it yet."

Looking for mathematics in your everyday life can help your child gain a better understanding of mathematical concepts. Thank you for your participation.

Sincerely,

Bubble Wrap Fish Pattern

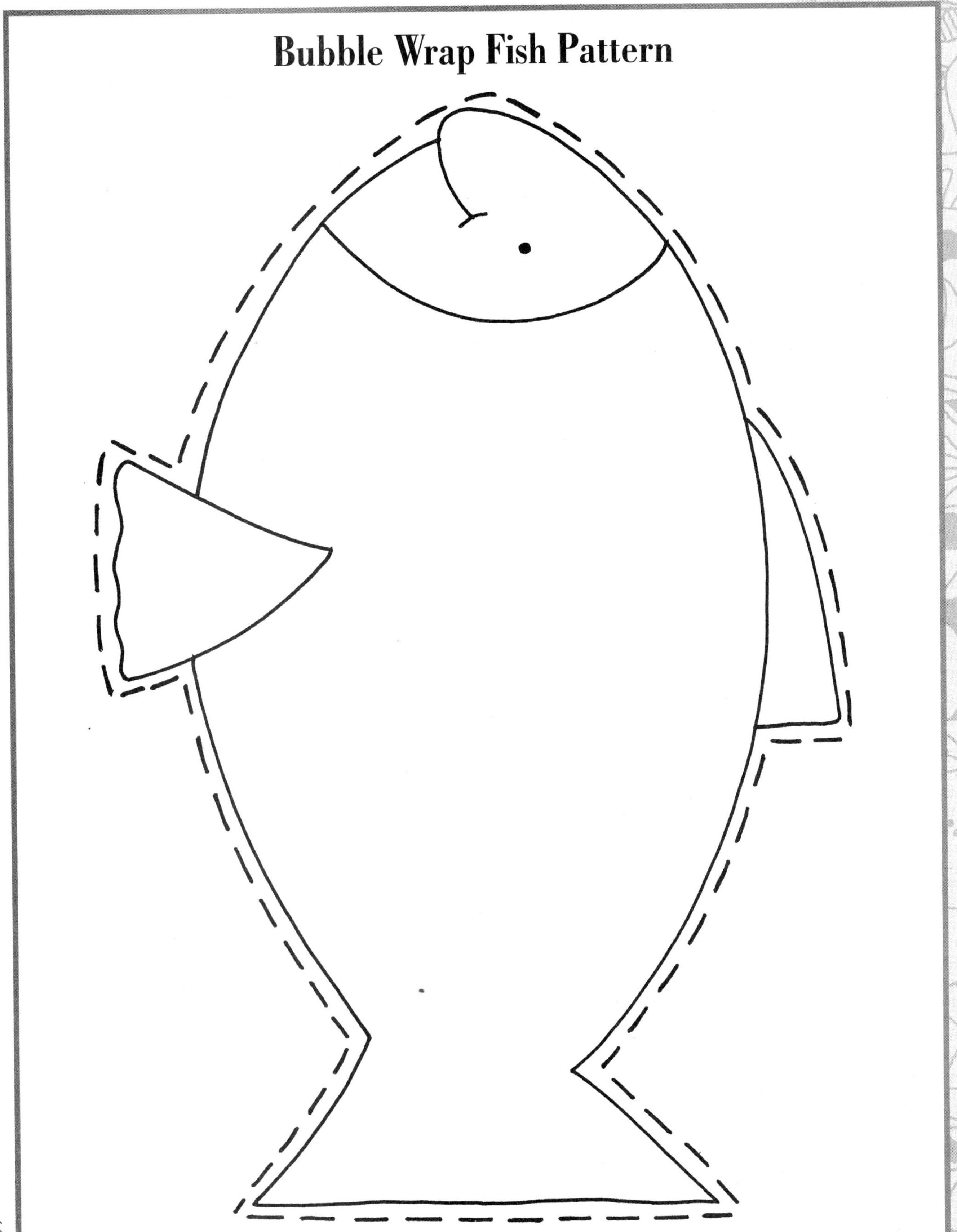

1	one
2	two
3	three
4	four

5	five
6	six
7	seven
8	eight

9	nine
10	ten
11	eleven
12	twelve

13	thirteen
14	fourteen
15	fifteen
16	sixteen

NUMBER CARDS

17	seventeen
18	eighteen
19	nineteen
20	twenty

Date:__________

Dear ______________________________,

Thank you for offering to contribute materials for our classroom.

Please send the materials to school with your child in a labeled plastic bag by

____.

This week, we are in need of the following:

____

____

____

____

____

Thank you,

VOCABULARY LIST

Suggested Math Vocabulary List

add
attribute
balance
calculator
category
chart
circle
classify
clock
collect
collection
color
compare
conclusion
cone
corner
count
cube
cylinder
data
day
design
divide
equal
equals
equal to
estimate
estimation
face
flip
foot
fraction
gather
geometry
graph
group
guess
half
hour
how many
inch
length
less
less than
line
longer
measure
minus
minute
month
more
more than
number
o'clock
observation
observe
ones
oval
organize
part
pattern
picture
plus
predict
probability
problem solve
quantity
record
rectangle
repeat
represent
ruler
same as
scale
second
shape
shapes
share
shorter
side
size
skip-counting
slide
sort
sphere
square
subtract
symbol
symmetry
tangram
telling time
tens
time
triangle
turn
volume
week
weigh
weight
whole
year

Suggested Math Literature List

Counting

Aylesworth, Jim. (1988). *One crow.* New York: Lippincott.
Bang, Molly. (1983). *Ten, nine, eight.* New York: Puffin Books.
Conover, Chris. (1976). *Six little ducks.* New York: Crowell.
Ehlert, Lois. (1990). *Fish eyes.* New York: Harcourt Brace.
Feelings, Muriel. (1971). *Moja means one.* New York: Dial Press.
Fleming, Denise. (1992). *Count.* New York: Holt.
Grossman, Virginia. (1991). *Ten little rabbits.* San Francisco: Chronicle Books.

Geometry

Carle, Eric. (1992). *Draw me a star.* New York: Philomel Books.
Embereley, Ed. (1996). *Picture pie.* Boston: Little, Brown and Company.
Hoban, Tana. (1974). *Circles, triangles, squares.* New York: Macmillan.
Hoban, Tana. (2000). *Cubes, cones, cylinders, and spheres.* New York: Greenwillow Books.
Hoban, Tana. (1970). *Shapes and things.* New York: Macmillan.
Shaw, Charles. (1947). *It looked like spilt milk.* New York: Harper.

Measurement

Allen, Pamela. (1980). *Mr. Archimedes' bath.* New York: Lothrop, Lee & Shepard Books.
Krauss, Ruth. (1974). *The carrot seed.* New York: Scholastic.
Lionni, Leo. (1960). *Inch by inch.* New York: Astor-Honor Inc.
Myfler, Rolf. (1962). *How big is a foot.* New York: Atheneum.

Probability

Anno & Nozaki. (1985). *Anno's hat tricks.* New York: Philomel Books.
London, Jonathan. (1992). *Froggy gets dressed.* New York: Penguin Books.
Wood, Audrey. (1989). *The napping house.* San Diego: Harcourt Brace Jovanovich.

Fractions

Giles, Jenny. (2004). *Two halves and four quarters.* Barrington, IL: Rigby.
Mathewa, Louise. (1979). *Gator pie.* New York: Dodd, Mead.
McMillan, Bruce. (1991). *Eating fractions.* New York: Scholastic.
Murphy, Stuart J. (1996). *Give me half!* New York: HarperCollins.

Sorting/Classifying

Carlson, Nancy. (2002). *Harriet's Halloween candy*. Minneapolis: Carolrhoda Books.

Hoban, Tana. (1987). *Is it red? Is it yellow? Is it blue?* New York: Greenwillow Books.

Murphy, Stuart J. (2000). *Dave's down-to-earth rock shop.* New York: HarperCollins.

Murphy, Stuart J. (2001). *Seaweed soup.* New York: HarperCollins.

Slobodkina, Esphyr. (1987). *Caps for sale.* New York: Scholastic.

Time

Tufuri, Nancy. (1984). *All year long.* New York: Puffin Books.

Anno, Mitsumasa. (1987). *Anno's sundial.* New York: Philomel Books.

Carle, Eric. (1977). *The grouchy ladybug.* New York: HarperCollins.

Carle, Eric. (1994). *The very hungry caterpillar.* New York: Philomel Books.

Burns, Marilyn. (1978). *This is a book about time.* Boston: Little, Brown and Company.

Hutchins, Pat. (1985). *You'll soon grow into them, Titch.* New York: Puffin Books.

Patterns

Carle, Eric. (1984). *The very busy spider.* New York: Philomel Books.

Blood, Charles, & Link, Martin. (1990). *The goat in the rug.* New York: Aladdin Books.

Giles, Jenny. (2004). *Making party hats.* Barrington, IL: Rigby.

Harris, Trudy. (2000). *Pattern fish.* Connecticut: Millbrook Press.

Graphing

Baylor, Byrd. (1977). *Guess who my favorite person is.* New York: Scribner.

Strinson, Kathy. (1982). *Red is best.* Toronto, Canada: Annick Press; Scarborough, Ontario: Distributed in Canada and the USA by Firefly Books.

Kellogg, Steven. (1977). *The mysterious tadpole.* New York: Dial Press.

Wildsmith, Brian. (2001). *Whose shoes?* San Diego: Harcourt.

Symmetry

Giles, Jenny. (2004). *Animal symmetry.* Barrington, IL: Rigby.

Giles, Jenny. *(2004). Making a butterfly.* Barrington, IL: Rigby.

Murphy, Stuart J. (2000). *Let's fly a kite.* New York: HarperCollins.

Addition/Subtraction

Giles, Jenny. (2004). *Five and five are ten.* Barrington, IL: Rigby.

Giles, Jenny. (2004). *Take two.* Barrington, IL: Rigby.

Giles, Jenny. (2004). *The take-away puppy.* Barrington, IL: Rigby.

Suggested Math Manipulative List

Attribute blocks
Balances and scales
Base ten blocks
Beans
Bear Counters
Bottle caps
Boxes
Bug counters
Buttons
Cardboard tubes
Calculators
Clothespins
Color tiles
Color cubes
Corks
Demonstration clocks
Dice
Flash cards
Frog counters
Geoboards
Geosolids
Golf tees
Keys
Linking cubes
Measuring cups and spoons
Number tiles
Nuts, bolts, screws
Old game pieces
Packaging peanuts
Paper clips
Paper plates
Pasta
Pattern blocks
Poker chips
Popsicle sticks
Puzzles
Rubber stamps
Rulers
Shells
Shoe boxes
Spinners
Stickers
String
Tape measures
Twist ties
Yarn

LITERACY CENTER ICONS

Reading/Writing Center

Math Center

Science Center

Art Center

Dramatic Play Center

Kids in the Kitchen Center

Web Sites

Math Standards
www.nctm.org/standards

Ladybug Activities
http://www.osr.state.ga.us/bestprac/math/M-11.htm
http://www.kiddyhouse.com/Teachers/Literature/grouch.html
http://www.vickiblackwell.com/lit/ladybug.html
http://www.smart-teachers.com/pdf/ladybugov.pdf

Math and Literature
http://www.mrsmcgowan.com/math/math_and_literature.htm

Tangrams
http://www.leon.k12.fl.us/Public/SabalPalm/tchrpages/grade4/tangram.htm
http://www.kidscom.com/games/tangram/tangram.html

Inchworms
http://www.reachoutmichigan.org/funexperiments/quick/inchworm/inching.html

Frogs
http://www.abcteach.com/index.html
http://www.flickit.com/frog.html

Math Activities
http://www.teach-nology.com/teachers/educational_technology/internet_in_class/students/math/

Fractions
http://www.aaamath.com/fra.html
http://www.coolmath4kids.com/lessons/

Rocks
http://www.rockhounds.com
http://www.irving.org/rocks
http://www.beakman.com/rock-candy/rock-candy.html

Telling Time
http://www.lil-fingers.com/games/time/index.html
http://www.primarygames.com/time/start.htm
http://www.kidsolr.com/earlychildhood/page4.html

Math Dictionary for Kids
http://www.amathsdictionaryforkids.com/

Professional Resources

Baker, A., & Baker, J. (1990). *Mathematics in progress.* Portsmouth, NH: Heinemann.

Baker, A., & Baker, J. (1991). *Raps and rhymes in math.* Portsmouth, NH: Heinemann.

Baratta-Lorton, M. (1972). *Workjobs: Activity-centered learning for early childhood education.* Menlo Park, CA: Addison-Wesley.

Baroody, A. (1989). *A guide to teaching mathematics in the primary grades.* Boston, MA: Allyn and Bacon.

Burk, D., Snider, A., & Symonds, P. (1988). *Box it or bag it mathematics: First-second teacher's resource guide.* Salem, OR: The Math Learning Center/Bassett Press.

Burns, M., & Tank, B. (1987). *A collection of math lessons from grades 1 through 3.* Math Solution Publications; White Plains, NY: Distributed by Cuisenaire Company of America.

Burns, M. (1982). *Math for smarty pants.* Boston, MA: Little, Brown and Company.

Charles, R., Lester, F., & O'Daffer, P. (1987). *How to evaluate progress in problem solving.* Reston,VA: NCTM.

Charles, R., & Silver, E. (1989). *The teaching and assessing of mathematical problem solving.* Reston,VA: NCTM.

Coates, G., & Stenmark, J. K. (1997). *Family math for young children.* University of California, Berkeley: Equals Publications.

Cutler, K. M., Gilkerson, D., & Parrott, S. (2003). Developing math games based on children's literature. *Young Children, 58*, 22-27.

Fromboluti, C. S., and Rinck, N. (1999). *Early childhood: Where learning begins.* Retrieved 08/14/03, from http://www.ed.gov/pubs/EarlyMath/index.html.

Griffiths, R., & Clyne, M. (1991). *Books you can count on: Linking mathematics and literature.* Portsmouth, NH: Heinemann.

Hellwig, S. J., Monroe, E. E., & Jacobs, J. S. (2000). Making informed choices: Selecting children's trade books for mathematics instruction. *Teaching Children Mathematics, 7*, 138-143.

McDuffie, A. R., & Young, T. (2003). Promoting mathematical discourse through children's literature. *Teaching Children Mathematics, 9*, 385-389.

Meagher, Sandy. (2003). Not your typical math books. *Teaching PreK-8, 33*, 56-57.

Moyer, P. S., (2000). Communicating mathematically: Children's literature as a natural connection. *The Reading Teacher, 54*, 246-255.

National Council for Teachers of Mathematics. (2000). Retrieved 08/14/03, from http://www.ed.gov/pubs/EarlyMath/index.html.

Readence, J. E., Moore, D. W., & Rickelman, R. J. (2000). *Prereading activities for content area reading and learning.* Delaware:International Reading Association.

Whitin, D.J., & Wilde, S. (1992). *Read any good math lately: Children's books for mathematical learning, K-6.* Portsmouth, NH: Heinemann.